ICE HOCKEY POEMS
2013-2023

by Lucy London

Published in Great Britain in August 2023 by Ice Hockey Review which is an imprint of Posh Up North Publishing, Beckenham Road, Wallasey.

The majority of the poems in this book have been previously published on Lucy – Poet In Residence Facebook Page - but they have not been published together in this layout before.

British Library cataloguing in publication data.
A catalogue record for this book is available from the British Library

ISBN: 978-1-909643-57-4

Front Cover Image:
Lucy London with referees Stephen French and Roy Ormes at a Women's Premier League match at Widnes, December 2018 (photo by Paul Breeze.)

Back Cover Image:
Lucy London in the Officials Booth at Planet Ice Widnes at the Laidler Division Play Offs, April 2019 (photo by Paul Breeze)

CONTENTS

Lucy London in the game officials' booth during the 2019 Laidler Play Off final (photo by David Tattum / DJT Ice Hockey Photos).

Lucy doing the match scoring at a Riverside Raiders game at Widnes during summer 2018 (Photo by Paul Breeze)

Lucy London – Poet In Residence

Lucy London was appointed honorary "Poet In Residence" for the Widnes Wild club in September 2017 and has since made it her mission to immortalise their exploits in verse.

She had previously watched ice hockey for a number of years at Peterborough, Altrincham, Blackburn and Blackpool / Cleveleys and has followed the Wild since moving closer to the area in 2015.

Lucy was an EIHA off-ice game official at Widnes for several seasons from 2017 to 2020, the match scorer for Riverside Raiders home games and has been the sponsor of the MVP awards for the Wild women's team for the past four seasons. Unfortunately, she has been laid low by poor health recently and is currently supporting from a distance.

Lucy is an experienced writer and broadcaster and has had two volumes of her own poems published as well as a song book, numerous short stories and various feature articles.

She has also become a bit of an authority on lesser known poetry of the First World War since being asked to put together an exhibition of women poets for the Wilfred Owen Story museum in Birkenhead back in 2012.

She has since edited and published numerous books on the subject of women poets, inspirational women and forgotten male poets of World War One and has staged exhibitions across the UK and in Ireland, France and the USA.

Back in September 2017, it was thought to be the first time that an ice rink had appointed a Poet In Residence and it is just another example that helps reinforce Widnes Wild's commitment to building strong links across the wider community.

Lucy London has a dedicated Facebook page for her poetry residency at Planet Ice Widnes and is keen to encourage other people to explore and develop their own artistic and literary talents.

You can follow her poetic musings on the goings on at Widnes at www.facebook.com/Lucy-Poet-In-Residence

And find information about Lucy's other First World War projects and other publications here:
http://femalewarpoets.blogspot.co.uk/

A cartoon version of Lucy by Manga Mark

Blackpool Seagulls Ice Hockey Team

I love the sound the seagulls make
As they follow the ships in their foaming wake
In their hunt for fish they dive and swoop
Wheeling and squealing as they loop the loop.

My favourite gulls are these on ice
I've seen them in action once or twice.
They play Ice Hockey at SubZero
In Cleveleys - you really ought to go,
If to a match you've not yet been
To be believed, it must be seen!
So get your skates on, get down to SubZero
And choose your Blackpool Seagulls hero.

I like to watch them dive and duck
As they chase the ever elusive puck
With crossing and checking and high sticks
The Seagulls are up to their usual tricks.

Go Blackpool Seagulls Ice Hockey Team
Bring us some silver in two thousand and thirteen!

Lucy London, Fleetwood, February/March 2013

Bruce Sims in his first game for Blackpool Seagulls since 1983 at the SubZero rink in Cleveleys in March 2013, with reigning Miss Blackpool Kim Braithwaite and her friend Georgina Young (Photo by Paul Breeze)

Background to The Sims Twins Poem

I have written poems for as long as I can remember - and I have watched ice hockey on and off since 1998 when Paul first took me to see the Peterborough Pirates play the Sheffield Steelers in a rather one sided game at Sheffield Arena - but I had never even thought about combining the two joys until 2013.

Paul was producing a charity match programme to celebrate the visit of a former Canadian player for Blackpool who was coming over to play in a game for the Seagulls after 30 years away and he asked me to write a poem about the Sims twins (Bruce and Brian) to put in it.

I had never seen the Sims twins play so he gave me few pointers and this is what I came up with.

Sims Twins Tribute

Those amazing, terrifying twins
Known as Brian and Bruce Sims
With flying skates and matching moustaches
For thirty years they've scared Defences
Scoring goals and winning matches,
Thrilling everyone who watches.
They came from Canada's far off land
To give the skating Brits a hand
Playing for Southampton and for Blackpool
When it comes to Ice Hockey they know every rule.
Let's hope they wow us for thirty years more
As goals for Blackpool Seagulls they score.

Lucy London, Meols, 7th March 2013

We met up with Bruce later on in his visit and had a nice long chat with him – and he told me how much he liked the poem!

Brian and Bruce Sims with fellow import Steve Currie at Blackpool Seagulls in 1982.

Bruce and Brian Sims with former Southampton team-mate Nick Drew in 2016 (Photo by Paul Breeze)

Lucy with Widnes Wild women's player Kat Garner #88
(Photo by Paul Breeze)

I love watching the Wild women's team play and am
always surprised at how they manage to look so graceful
with all that kit on!

My sister was a professional ballet dancer and that is
another discipline where a lot of hard work and training
behind the scenes goes on to make the final product look
smooth and almost effortless…

Here's a poem that I wrote at one of the first Wild
women's games that I saw:

Ballet Shoes and Skating Boots

*(Started at the Ice Hockey Match Widnes Wild women v.
Slough Phantoms, 28th February 2016, Silver Blades Ice
Rink, Widnes).*

Like ballet shoes, the skaters' boots are laced and worn
with care
And for every discipline, they need a different pair
For speed or hockey, dance on ice or even figure skating
The blade and boot are different, as is of course the
lacing.

With ballet there are character boots, shoes with blocks
and more
Almost as hard as ice are the wood blocks on the floor
Pirouettes or passing pucks both keep you on your toes
Your equipment is expensive – that's where the money
goes!

Whether it's the ice pad or "treading the boards"
The referee's shrill whistle or Tchaikowsky's rousing
chords,
Dedication, commitment, practice and passion
Are all important for the stars but so is following fashion.

Lucy London, 8th September 2016.

SEASON 2017/18

I am really excited to have been named honorary Poet In Residence for the Silver Blades Ice Rink in Widnes.

Here's an initial offering!

Silver Blades Ice Rink, Widnes

Widnes Town's in Lancashire* on the banks of the Mersey River
Silver Blades Ice Rink has a fantastic ice skating scene
Don't forget to dress warmly – we don't want you to shiver
The Ice Rink is home to several ice hockey teams
Widnes Wild Women and Widnes Wild Men, the Raiders, the Huskies and more
Come and watch a match even if you've never been before.
No matter what the weather, Silver Blades has the blues on the run
A café and bar, a warm welcome and lots of fun
From skating for fun to training for sport, they've a poet and chaplain too
There's something for all at the Silver Blades Rink – we look forward to seeing you.

*Historically Lancashire – now in Cheshire....

Lucy London - 25th September 2017

Pukka Penguin on the ice during a period break (photo by David Tattum)

Pukka Penguin's Poem

Three cheers for Pukka the Widnes Penguin
We love him 'cos he's so very genuine.
Pukka the Penguin's the Widnes Wild Mascot
He clears the ice and does such a lot.
Oh! Pukka Penguin we love you,
We think it's clever what you do
The way you skate and clear the ice
You wave to us - that's really nice.
And when it comes to Chuck-a-duck
We have a go and try out luck.
So thank you Pukka for all you do
Pukka Penguin we love you!

Lucy London - September 2017

Lucy with Doug Brown of RTL who were the Wild's main sponsors from 2015 to 2018 (Photo by Paul Breeze)

I had a nice chat with Doug Brown at the game on Sunday and he was very interested in my poetry projects. His company RTL are the Widnes Wild main sponsors and I was moved to pen a few lines about them:

RTL

RTL, RTL, that name certainly rings a bell.
If you go down to Warrington Town you're sure to find RTL
They recycle computers and do some up to sell.
You're always sure of good value,
So pick up a bargain today
From Recycle Technology Limited
Who are showing the world the way.

Lucy London, 1st October 2017

Lucy the poet comparing warm headgear with Andrew Shutt
(Photo by Paul Breeze)

I have written a poem about Andrew Shutt but he sent me a really good limerick after the Altrincham Aces game and, as that is time-related, I thought I'd post that for now and share my poem about him another time. So here it is….!

There is a team called the WILD,
Who play hockey but not very mild,
When playing the Aces
They touched all the bases
A two one win, how we smiled

By Andrew Shutt, 13th October 2017

ANDY SHUTT

Andy with his wild head gear
Always ready with a joke and a smile
For Widnes Wild you'll hear him cheer
For them he'll go the extra mile.
He collects the rubbish in Interval Time
I really hope he likes my rhyme.

By Lucy London, October 2017

And here's a ditty from Paul on the same subject:

I said to Andy: "I like your Hat"
"It's a HEAD-DRESS" he said
So that was that...

And another one on a different subject:

Rovena's from Nebraska
If don't know where that is
You can ask her...

*Lucy in Poet's Corner during the Wild v Telford match
(photo by Paul Breeze)*

Here's a poem that I wrote during the Widnes Wild v Telford Tigers match on Sunday. This is actually the first time that I have written poem DURING a match and I was very much inspired by the cheerleaders.

Telford Tigers, Widnes Wild,

Telford Tigers, Widnes Wild,
Oliver's Army not meek and mild.
Come on Widnes, let's see your wild side
You've hockey skills it's a shame to hide.
Let's go Widnes – score some more
What we want is goals galore!
Listen to the Cheerleaders, Listen to the Crowd
Hear them cheering clear and loud:
"Come on Widnes, let's go Wild".

Lucy London, 29.10.2017 - with grateful thanks to Lynne from Sheffield.

It's really lovely to see all the decorations that have been put up around the Widnes rink for the festive period. I had an amazing experience before the game against Hull the other weekend when I noticed one of those "sprinkle around" table glitter decorations lying on the ground right in front of me where I was sitting and I was moved to write these lines:

The Star *(Written at Silver Blades Ice Rink on Sunday, 26th November 2017)*

At Silver Blades in Widnes town,
Where Widnes Wild* can be found,
A Christmas tree and Santa's sleigh
All on a cold, wet winter day.
While the teams warm up, I looked around
And saw a brightness on the ground,
Perhaps left over from some party treat
A tiny star trampled on by passing feet.
It seemed to me to be there to remind us
Of the star-bright message of Christmas.

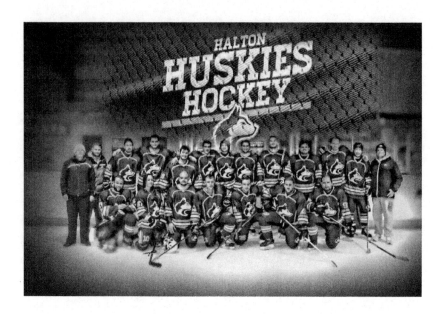

I was very keen to hear how the Halton Huskies team were getting on away at Grimsby last night and it was great that Matt Lloyd was able to go the game and post match updates on Facebook!

Go Huskies!
(03.02.2018 Grimsby Stormers 26 – Halton Huskies)3

Well done to the Huskies Ice Hockey Team
You did your best and I know you are all very keen
But it's not all about winning – although that is great –
It's much more important to participate.
Tonight you played well and tried very hard
Playing a big fish on a small pond in their own backyard.
So heads up Halton Huskies, don't be sad and blue
Go Huskies! Go Huskies! You will soon win through.

Lucy London, 3rd February 2018

Looking forward to Sunday when they are two games on at Widnes: Wild v Coventry in the NIHL at 5.30 and Halton Huskies v Whitley rec game at 8.30pm

Back To Back Matches

Back-to-back matches. Oh! What a treat!
Widnes Wild v. Coventry Blaze, Halton Huskies v Whitley Bay Sharks.
You'd better get there early to make sure you get a seat.
It'll be interesting to see which team has the loudest barks.

L.L. 15.02.2018

ANDY SHUTT (version 2)

Andrew with his Wild head gear
Always ready with a joke and a smile
For Widnes Wild you'll hear him cheer
For them he'll go the extra mile.
You will find him keeping Wild time
And if you look closely you may see him mime.

Lucy London, 8th April 2018

Looking forward to the Laidler Play Offs next weekend, which are being held in Widnes for the first time:

Play Off Weekend

Welcome to Planet Ice in Merseyside's Widnes town
Where Widnes Wild are sponsored by RTL's Doug Brown.
Well done to all the teams who have reached the Play-Off games
Give me a minute and I'll tell you all their names:
Hull Jets, Telford Tigers, Widnes Wild and Sutton Sting
Let's see what results the Play-Offs bring.

LL 1.4.2018

Here are few lines I jotted down during the play-off final between Sutton and Widnes:

Widnes Wild v. Sutton Sting

At half way through
The score was 3 : 2
Counting down, 9 minutes left
Who can get the puck in the net?
Random Lines
The interesting thing
About a sting
Is that bees lose the lot
Whereas wasps do not.

Lucy London, 15th April 2018

I had a great time at the Laidler Play Offs held at Widnes last weekend - and it was nice to see the Wild win the trophy in front of their home fans:

NIHL Play-Off Weekend, Planet Ice, Widnes, 14th – 15th April 2018

The Laidler Play-Offs at Planet Ice were a wonderful event
Here's to the backroom girls and boys who you don't often see
They all work extremely hard and have a terrific commitment
Their dedication and attention to detail were very clear to me.
Well played to all the Hockey teams and their adoring fans,
And thanks to all the referees without whom no game's complete -
Hardy, Rodger, Stanley, Fraley, Wang and Hands -
And thanks to all the volunteers who work behind the scenes
They all ensured that that weekend will be very hard to beat.
They make sure that Widnes Wild are the very best of teams.

Lucy London - 17th April 2018

SUMMER 2018

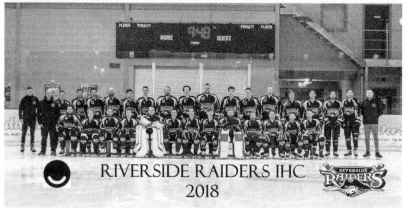

Riverside Raiders team photo 2018 (Photo by Mike Teinert)

Recreational Ice Hockey

Soon
Will the high summer of our Wild content
Be turned into glorious chill winter
At the Widnes Planet Ice Rink
And Ice Hockey teams
Will fulfil my waking dreams
Of completing score sheets
And handing out sweets,
And understanding signals from referees -
Ormes and Wells and the Humpreys.
And Alway, Wang and Twell
They will all cast their spell -
Halton Huskies and Riverside Raiders,
Anders, Campbell, Povall and French
And all the players on the Bench …

Lucy London, 13th March 2018 – revised 30th July 2018

I am really looking forward to the Riverside Raiders game tomorrow at Planet Ice Widnes when they play the Steel City Hawks in the Summer Classic Cup. Face off is 4.30pm and admission is free!

Raiders Are Back

Riverside Raiders
I'm so glad you're back
The Wild are great
but there's something they lack

Once more unto the fray, dear Friends,
let us see what this Season brings
As the Widnes Wild ice hockey season ends,
so the Rec. Hockey Season begins.

Riverside Raiders

My heart's with Rec Ice Hockey, more so than the Wild*
When it comes to Rec Hockey, I'm just like a child
The atmosphere's different – a bit more laid back
Though you wouldn't think it when the Raiders attack.
Good luck Riverside Raiders as you defend your title
Concentrate and keep positive, for me that is vital.
Play up, play the game – I really hope you win
Play up, play the game but stay out of the sin bin.

Lucy London, 31st March 2018

*PS I love the Wild too, obviously – this is just poetic licence based on (hommage to…) an earlier, more famous, work by somebody else…!

Lucy and Paul after helping out at Raiders game during 2018
(Photo by Geoff White)

Riverside Raiders, Pirates of the north west
Of Ice Hockey Teams you are one of the best
Sometimes your excellence is put to the test,
So here are some sweets to give you some zest.

LL, June 2018

Riverside Raiders don't dehydrate -
That's something we would really hate -
So here's some water for you to drink
And keep hydrated while you're in the rink.

LL

Riverside Raiders, the Widnes-based Team,
our Ice Hockey heroes so bold
They remind me a lot, as they skate on by, of the
swashbuckling pirates of old.
Thank you for letting me keep the score card for
Raiders' matches at home
And for putting up so gallantly with yet another daft
poem.

Lucy London, June 2018

Halton Huskies, Ice Hockey Hounds
Your on-ice enthusiasm knows no bounds
And now, before more icing feats
We hope you will enjoy these sweets.

LL, June 2018

Riverside Raiders, I may watch other teams
But only the Raiders haunt my dreams.
Riverside Raiders, when I can't sleep
(Usually after a Raiders' match,
Which are always so exciting to watch)
I don't bother counting sheep
But think of rhymes to put with the Raiders' sweets.

LL

Bunny, Alice and Archie watching the ice hockey at Planet Ice Widnes
(Photo by Paul Breeze)

Bunny and Alice and Archie

Bunny and Alice and Archie went to visit Planet Ice
In Widnes Town in Cheshire – they thought it was very nice.
Archie's cousin Charlie works at the ice rink
They make a handsome pair – what do you all think?
The Pals watched the ice hockey and thought it was great fun
At Planet Ice in Widnes there's something for everyone.

Lucy London, 17th June 2018

Here is Archie with cousin Charlie. Please note: no ice hockey players were harmed during the taking of these photos… (Photo by Paul Breeze)

I posted this poem before but realised that I had missed off some of the regular local match officials, so thought I'd better give it a tweak before the Summer Classic Cup gets under way tomorrow:

Ice Hockey

Soon
Will the high summer of our Wild content
Be turned into glorious chill winter
In the Planet Ice Rink
In Widnes.
And Ice Hockey teams
Will fulfil my waking dreams
Of completing score sheets
And handing out sweets,
And understanding signals from referees -
Ormes and Wells and Humphreys.
Along with Wang and Twell
They will all cast their spell -
And Anders,
Halton Huskies and Riverside Raiders,
And Campbell, Povall and French
And all the players on the Bench …

Lucy London, 13th March 2018 – revised 30th March 2018

Sledge Hockey

Don't fret the Season's over
For some it's just begun
Come and support Sledge Hockey
At Planet Ice on Sun (day...)

(22nd April 2018, Face Off 16.30 – entry free).

Sixth Of May

Looking ahead to Sunday, the sixth of May
Flintshire Phantoms and Riverside Raiders play
In the Summer Cup Raiders won last year
If you're an ice hockey fan come along and cheer.

Halton Huskies, Ice Hockey Hounds
Your on-ice enthusiasm knows no bounds
And now, before more icing feats
We hope you will enjoy these sweets.

LL, June 2018

Two Games Tomorrow

Calling ice hockey fans
a word to the wise
On Sunday, 17th June
in Widnes at Planet Ice.
There are back to back matches
Oh! what a treat
When Raiders and Huskies
their opponents meet.

Lucy London 16th June 2018

Fed up with football? Feeling the heat?
Head down to Widnes – you're in for a treat.
Planet Ice are hosting a Rec. Hockey tourn-a-ment
Mikey Gilbert's in charge – it'll be a great event.

Lucy London, 5th July 2018

Lucy and Paul in the Officials Box at the Widnes Rec Tournament, July 2018

Widnes Rec Tournament

Rec. Hockey organised by Mikey Gilbert held over last
weekend
Took me a week to recover from - I will not pretend
The pace was fast, the games were great at Widnes
Planet Ice Rink
If you want to find out what happened, you will have to
follow this link:
www.icehockeyreview.co.uk

Lucy London, 14th July 2018

Above: Volunteers at the Widnes Rec Tournament in July 2018 Terry Gary, Paul Breeze, Lucy London, Colin Ellis & Geoff White (Photo by Mikey Gilbert)

Left: Lucy and Paul at the Rec Tournament, July 2018 (Photo by Geoff White)

Season 2018/19

Looking forward to the Widnes Wild v Sheffield Senators game tomorrow - here are a few lines to get things going for the new season:

Widnes Wild this season
are sponsored by YKK
The new team's looking great as well
Can't wait to see them play
At Planet Ice in Widnes
Face Off 5.30 on Sunday.

LL 7th September 2018

VIP guests from new sponsors YKK at the Wild game v against Sheffield
(Photo by Geoff White)

It was great to see the sponsors from YKK at the game at Widnes on Sunday – and what game it was – with a 4-3 to the Wild in their first league game of the season!

notjustazip

It's a pleasure to watch the Widnes Wild
as they zip around the pad
Not just a zip, not just a team,
so much fun to be had!
See the YKK-sponsored ice hockey team
at Planet Ice in Widnes
YKK make different fasteners
and are a world-renowned business.

Lucy London, 10th September 2018

Here are a few new lines about the ice hockey at Widnes:
Widnes Wild play Bradford Bulldogs
23rd September 2018

Face off is at five thirty –
get your tickets! Don't be late!
Let's hear it for the new Wild Team
who are all under fifteen
They played their first match against Blackburn,
a more experienced team

Lucy London, 21st Sept 2018

Not Just A Zip Maker

Not just a zip maker - more a leading light
Not just an ice rink – a place for family fun
And really good food - so why don't you come
Catch a Widnes Wild Ice Hockey match on Sunday
night?

LL 3.10.2018

Colin Ellis with the British Para Ice Hockey League play off cup at the Sledge final at Widnes in September 2018 (Photo by Paul Breeze)

Thank You Colin

Thank you Colin
I'm really wild about Colin's photos –
Colin's brilliant – with his videos
Of Wild matches and his Monday show
On Halton Community Radio.
Colin Ellis for all you do
We'd like to say a huge THANK YOU.

Lucy London, 2nd October 2018

Janet Pritchard from main sponsors YKK presents a large cuddly toy to support the Christmas teddy donations to Wild community co-ordinator Andrew Wycherley. Gill Gillingham, Paul and Lucy can be seen in the officials' box (Photo by Wild Twitter)

A few lines that came to me during the period breaks in the game against Coventry on Sunday:

Let's have applause and a very loud cheer
For the people whose job it is to clear
The ice pad after every game
Without them it wouldn't be the same.
THANK YOU!

LL, 2nd December 2018

Wild Things you make our hearts sing
What better present could Santa bring
Than a walk on the side that's Wild
For a really Wild child.

LL 2nd December 2018

Let's Hear It For The Referees

Let's hear it for the referees -
Whose job it is to keep the peace
And try to ensure that in every match
The players are kept up to scratch.

Lucy London, 17th December 2018

Teddy Toss

The folk at Widnes Planet Ice
Are very kind and very nice
They went through all the Teddy drop
And took the best – the cream of the crop -
To Halton Hospital and Alder Hey
For the children to have on Christmas Day.
The second hand teddies don't get thrown out -
And this is brilliant without a doubt -
They get taken to the local dogs' home
So no doggies are left with none.
Thank you to all at Planet Ice Widnes
And to you all a very Happy Christmas.

Lucy London, 20th December 2018

Planet Ice At Christmas

No need to go to Lapland to look for winter fun
Planet Ice in Widnes is the place for everyone
Hire a penguin, learn to skate
Learn ice hockey – it's not too late
Skate after school, Junior Disco too
Lots of fun for me and you.
On Sunday the 2nd of December
There's a Teddy Drop – please remember.

Lucy London, 25th November 2018.

Christmas jumpers, Christmas hats
A Prize for the best dressed family that's
What's on offer on Sunday in Widnes
At Planet Ice, celebrating Christmas.
p.s. there's an ice hockey match too.

Lucy London, 13th December 2018

Mikey Gilbert (left) and Janet Pritchard from YKK (right) deliver donate toys to Alder Hay Hospital

The folk at Widnes Planet Ice
Are very kind and very nice
They went through all the Teddy drop
And took the best – the cream of the crop -
To Halton Hospital and Alder Hey
For the children to have on Christmas Day.

The second hand teddies don't get thrown out -
And this is brilliant without a doubt -
They get taken to the local dogs' home
So no doggies are left with none.
Thank you to all at Planet Ice Widnes
And to you all a very Happy Christmas.

Lucy London, 20th December 2018

Penalty boxes and officials booth all packed out. Photo courtesy of YKK Widnes Wild's excellent Twitter account....

Widnes Wild Volunteers

Let's have three loud and rousing cheers
For all the Widnes Wild Volunteers.
They don't share the players' spotlight
They work away mainly out of sight.
They help out at every Wild home game –
Without them things would not be the same.

Lucy London, 22nd December 2018

Noël à Planet Ice, Widnes

Les étoiles dansent sur la
surface
Eteincellant de la glace
Là-bas dans le coin,
Un petit sapin
Et un grand St. Nicolas,
Le Saint Patron
Des Enfants,
Me rappellent
Que c'est bientôt Noël -
Ce Soir,
Dans la patinoire.

At Planet Ice in Widnes
Tonight
Reflections of light
Make the surface of the ice pad
Seem almost as though it had
A thousand stars dancing there.
Santa Claus - Patron Saint of
children everywhere –
Keeps watch over all and a
Christmas tree
In the corner I see
Reminding me
It's almost Christmas.

Lucy London, le 16 décembre 2018

Wild player Danny Bullock receives the MVP award from Halton Councillor Andrea Wall (Photo by Geoff White)

Happy New Year to Widnes Wild
Who we haven't seen at home for quite a while
On Sunday they played an exciting match
Against Sheffield Senators – a joy to watch.
When the Wild win the fans holler for more
But we love to watch Wild whatever the score.
Our very own Councillor Andrea Wall
Presented the MVP awards.

Lucy London, 13th January 2019.

No need to miss out on any Wild ice action
The Wild Women's Team have an ice hockey match on
Sunday January 20th twenty nineteen
Come along and watch if you've never seen
Widnes Wild Women's Ice Hockey Team.

Face off 5.30 pm

When you go to an ice hockey match
Try, if you can, to remember to watch
For the whereabouts of the flying puck
If it comes your way, remember to duck…

Lucy London, 27th January 2019

Ollie Barron (Photo by David Tattum / DJT Photos)

We're Oliver's Army –
We're not Barmy –
This isn't cricket
Ice Hockey's just the ticket
We're all Wild –
Widnes Wild!

if you go down to Planet Ice in Widnes on Sunday,
after your visit to Sheffield,
you'll be able to see the Widnes Wild Women's Ice
Hockey Team's
home game against Chelmsford

Lucy London, 5th February 2019

Shannon Holt with Lucy and George III (he's the monkey...) picking a Chuck a Duck duck at a Wild game (Photo by Paul Breeze)

Shannon

Here's Shannon who sells Widnes Wild's Chuck a Duck. Why not have a go - it's easier than throwing a hockey puck.
Shannon's learning ice hockey and we really hope one day
To present Shannon with a Player Award like the one that's on display.

Lucy London, 11th February 2019

Widnes Wild players and match volunteers celebrate the Laidler Division title win in March 2019 (Photo by Geoff White)

W - ell done the Wild
I - n winning the Laidler Division Championship Trophy
L - ooking forward to the Play Offs
D - own at Planet Ice in Widnes over Easter Weekend.

Ok, it doesn't rhyme. It's a different form of poem...!

Lucy London, March 2019

Let's have a cheer for Widnes Ice Hockey Development Teams -
The Under 9s, Under 13s and Under Fifteens.
Hats off to Mickey Gilbert, who's in charge of Development
These are the players of the future so it's time and effort well spent.
Thank you to all the players and to the parents too
None of this would be possible if it weren't for all of you.

Lucy London, 23rd March 2019

Match officials Chris Wells, Simon Anders and Josh Humphreys at a summer rec game at Widnes (Photo by David Law Photography)

Lucy presents the MVP award to Wild women's player Liz Loss after the home game against Bracknell (photo by Paul Breeze)

Ormes and Twell and Josh Humphreys
Were the Match Officials – Referees -
When the Widnes Wild Women played the Bracknell Fire Bees.
Here are the photos of the M V Ps.
Lucy London, 9th April 2019

Oh what a shame!
We can't make today's Huskies game.
If ONLY we had known before –
You know how much I love to keep score.
Lucy London, 14th April 2019

The Wild in action against Slough Jets in the Division 2 National Championship game at Coventry – they lost 7-1 (photo by Carl Bungay)

Come on Widnes Wild – let's concentrate.
Though disappointing, Coventry did demonstrate
The Wild function best when they are a Team
Let's prepare for the Play Offs and make that Trophy gleam…

Lucy London, 15th April 2019

The Wild team and staff celebrate winning the Laidler Play Off final for the third time in a row (Photo by Paul Breeze)

WELL DONE
WIDNES WILD ONES
That made up
for not having Hot Cross Buns!

Lucy London, 21st April 2019

Summer 2019

The Widnes Wild women's team (Photo by Geoff White)

If watching ice hockey is how you get your kicks
Come to Planet Ice in Widnes for your regular fix.
Widnes Wild Women and all the Rec. Hockey Teams
Are playing through the summer at Widnes' ice palace of
dreams.

Lucy London, 21st April 2019

Good luck to the Riverside Raiders as they travel to the
Dee
To face the Flintshire Phantoms. I can't wait to see
The Raiders back in action at Widnes Planet Ice
They've a charity match on 26th May, so come along
don't think twice!

Lucy London, 5th May 2019

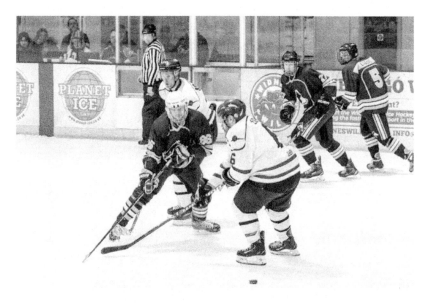

Paul and Lucy in the officials' box at the Halton Huskies v Coventry Spitfires game in March 2018 (Photo by David Law Photography)

Halton Huskies – WTF?

Did we do
Something to upset you
Last Season, Halton Huskies?
If so, please accept our apologies.

We always do our very best to keep the score,
Do the music and announcements and more,
Write up match reports for everyone to read
For all the Planet Ice in Widnes Ice Hockey Teams.

Lucy and Paul, 2nd May 2019

Gill Gillingham at the 2019 Laidler Play Offs at Widnes
(Photo by David Tattum / DJT Ice Hockey Photos)

Happy Birthday to Gill Gillingham.

The Gillinghams at Planet Ice, Widnes
Three cheers for the Gillinghams – Ice Hockey family
The Wild would be tame without you three.
Gill Gillingham's in charge of the electronic game card
She must be clever – this looks very hard.
Dick Gillingham helps in many ways;
For instance, he always takes care
To ensure the iced pucks are ready and there.
Mark Gillingham's retiring as the coach with Widnes Wild
We met them first on the Coast known as Fylde.

Lucy London, Poet in Residence, 5th May 2019

Mike Clancy unveiled as the new Wild Head Coach in May 2019
(Photo by Paul Breeze)

Heartfelt thanks to Ollie Barron, hero of the day,
As we say farewell to Wild's player coach and wave him
on his way.

Welcome to Mike Clancy, Widnes new Head Coach -
We look to you for leadership as the new season we
approach.

Lucy London, 12th May 2019

The song Lucy wrote for you Widnes Wild Women
is what we are hoping to play
As you take to the ice against Sheffield Shadows
at Planet Ice on Sunday.
Good luck Widnes Wild Women!

Lucy London 14th May 2019

Riverside Raiders Charity Match versus Trafford Thunder
On Sunday 26th May – who will win I wonder?
But it's not the winning that's important – this is a charity
match
With lots of chances to raise funds for Christies for those
who come and watch.

Sunday, 26th May 2019 Face Off 4.30 p.m. Admission
Free.

*Riverside Raiders and Trafford Thunder players together after the charity
match in aid of Christie Hospital (Photo by Paul Breeze)*

Yesterday's Match

Yesterday's match was fantastic – thanks to everyone who came
And to all of those who contributed to the success of the game
Organised by Howard Hughes, who deserved his MVP
To all the ice hockey players who played a fine match for all to see
To Sue Cartlidge and Shannon Holt for sterling work with the raffle and the cake
Ensuring that for The Christie Charity a generous contribution we could make.
Thanks to Carl for penalty box help and to Stacey for doing the clock
And to Paul Breeze for announcements and music to make us rock
To Colin Ellis for all his help and for his fantastic game videos
(And of course for Time to go Wild, Colin's amazing radio shows)
To all the staff at Planet Ice in Widnes behind the scenes on match days
And last but not least to the ice hockey players who continue to amaze
And Oh Dear Me, I almost forgot to thank the referees…

Apologies to anyone I have left out.

Lucy London. 27th May 2019

Go Raiders!

Riverside Raiders, Riverside Raiders, Pirates of the ice
When it comes to Ice Hockey you don't need my advice!
To tell the truth I haven't yet come back down to earth
After the charity match on 26th May – now let's see
what you're worth.
GO RAIDERS!

Lucy London, 7th June 2019

Lucy and Paul in the officials' box (photo by Geoff White)

Riverside Raiders v. Flintshire Phantoms, Planet Ice, Widnes, Sunday, 9th June 2019

It's that time of year again
When some folk start to moan and complain -
No more ice hockey till the end of summer
But I've not heard of anything dumber.
If you really love the game
You'll support Rec. Hockey just the same
So come on down
To Widnes Town
On Sunday the 9th of June
Face Off 4.30 in the afternoon.

Lucy London, 7th June 2019

Riverside Raiders v Flintshire Phantoms at Widnes
(Photo by Andrew Shutt)

Thanks For An Exciting Match

Thanks to the Raiders and Phantoms for an exciting
match
Thanks to all those who came along to watch
Thanks to Paul for music, announcements & the stuff he
writes
For the local newspaper and for the websites
Thanks to Andy Shutt for his fantastic photos
Thanks to Colin Ellis for his awesome videos
Thanks to Howard Smith for doing the clock
Thanks to Rosie for her help with the Penalty Box
Thanks to the staff behind the scenes at Planet Ice
For ensuring that all events there are simply ACE.
And thanks as well to the Referees
Whose signals I now see with greater ease.

Lucy London, 10th June 2019

Blackburn Buccaneers v Riverside Raiders at Deeside
(Photo by Paul Breeze)

Raiders and Buccaneers in the Dragons' Den
Will the Raiders ice their player called Ben?
Saturday, the 15th of June 2-0-1-9
Face off 5 pm - that is the time.
The place is Deeside Leisure Centre
Queensferry, Flintshire.

Lucy London, 13th June 2019

Paul volunteered to do the music but found
At Deeside Rink there was no sound.
For the Raiders versus Buccaneers match
Which, he said, was great to watch.
Coming back from 3 : 0 to equalise
The Raiders only lost on penalties.
Well played Raiders!

Lucy London, 15th June 2019

On Sunday, Riverside Raiders and Shropshire Huskies
go head to head –
Playing ice hockey must surely be more fun than pulling
a sled.
I double dare all Widnes Wild Fans to come along on
Sunday and watch
And let me know afterwards what you think of a Raiders'
match.

Lucy London, 17th June 2019

Riverside Raiders player Ben Donkin
(Photo by Davd Tattum / DJT Ice Hockey Photos)

The Donkin Song

The Riverside Raiders' player Ben Donkin
Asked Paul to play a special song in
Widnes Planet Ice when Raiders score.
To hear the song more often, Raiders, you just need to
score more!

Lucy London, 23rd June 2019

Well done to The Riverside Raiders Widnes Ice Hockey Team
Who beat the Shropshire Huskies 10 : 8 yesterday e'een.
We look forward to seeing the Raiders at home in the Summer Cup
Well done everybody – great work – keep it up, keep it up.

Lucy London, 25th June 2019

Riverside Raiders what am I to do?
Sleepless, I'm dreaming up verses to
Go with the sweets I offer to you.

Lucy London, 8th July 2019.

With all the ice in the rink,
Wouldn't you think
There'd be some water to drink!
Here's a drop of water
For a thirsty Riverside Raider.

Lucy London, 8th July 2019

Ice hockey is my passion - as you can guess from my
various lines,-
But at the rink there are on offer many other disciplines
So get on down to Widnes Planet Ice and find your own
cool passion
From beginners' ice hockey – all ages – there's every
kind of lesson.

Lucy London, 10th July 2019

A life on the ocean wave? No fear! We prefer to skate -
Two sets of pirates head to head on Sunday – we can't
wait.
Riverside Raiders are home to Blackburn Buccaneers
So don't hold back – for both the teams let's hear all the
cheers.

Lucy London, 11th July 2019

Wyre Seagulls in action at the SubZero rink in Cleveleys in December 2011
(Photo by Paul Breeze)

Wyre Seagulls

Wyre Seagulls Ice Hockey Team, get your sleeves rolled up
Tomorrow you face Flintshire Phantoms in the Summer Classic Cup
Because the Blackburn Planet Ice Rink isn't finished yet
The Seagulls are at home at Widnes - but you all knew that, I bet.

Lucy London, 26th July 2019

(We first saw the Wyre Seagulls play on 17th December 2011 in Cleveleys, so have bit of a soft spot for them...)

Season 2019/20

Photo by Hannah Walker

Widnes Wild come out to play
Against Altrincham Aces – home and away.
An ice rink is a cool place every day
(But especially when it's hot like today.)

Altrincham Aces v. Widnes Wild - Face Off 5.30pm,
Planet Ice Altrincham, Sunday 25th August 2019
Widnes Wild play Altrincham Aces
Great to see old and new faces
Wild're at home on 1st September
A date you really need to remember.

Face Off 5.30pm Widnes Wild v. Altrincham Aces,
Planet Ice, Widnes, Sunday, 1st September 2019

Widnes Wild, Widnes Wild, intrepid band of men
We cheer for you, shout loud for you and we remember
when
How proud we felt when you lifted those cups and hope
you do it again.

LL 7.9.2019

I've never know time to go so fast
Nearly a week since Sunday last
When Wild played a very exciting game -
With thanks to everyone who came.
The Wild's new season faces off Hurray!
Against Sheffield Senators at home on Sunday.
15th September 2019 5.30 p.m. Planet Ice Widnes

Lucy London, 13th September 2019

Stick'n'Step are a Mersey-side Charity
They help youngsters who've Cerebral Palsy
YKK-sponsored Widnes Wild's a Mersey-side Ice Hockey
Team
Each Season they support a Charity and do lots for the
local scene.

The YKK-sponsored Widnes Wild ice hockey team whose
home base is Planet Ice Widnes, are supporting
Stick'n'Step for the 2019-2020 NIHL Laidler Division
Season.

Three cheers for Widnes Wild and for Stick'n'Step

30 August 2019
Lucy - Poet in Residence Planet Ice, Widnes

On Saturday, 14th September 2019, a first ever UK taster event for visually impaired people was held at Planet Ice in Widnes, to give people a chance to try ice hockey. (Photo by Hannah Walker)

Planet Ice in Widnes, on the banks of the River Mersey,
Is surely the brightest Planet in our Galaxy
They hold the most amazing events for all the family.

Lucy London, 16th Sept 2019

Puck drop to start off the Wild women's 2019/20 season
(Photo by Paul Breeze)

We wish you well Widnes Wild Women as you ice against Solway
In your first home match this season - we know you played them away.
Widnes Wild Women – it will be interesting to see
How the Team gel together and who wins the MVP.

Lucy London, 21st September 2019

*Widnes Wild women players Catherine Fell, Sav Sumner, Emma Pearson &
Kat Garner (Photo by Paul Breeze)*

No ice hockey on Sunday? Don't sit at home and moan
For Widnes Wild Women's Team are at home
No need to miss out on the action or simply hang around
Face Off is at 5.30 and admission is just a pound.

Widnes Wild Women v. Sheffield Shadows in their first
Women's Division One North League Game of the
Season - Planet Ice Widnes. Face Off 5.30 p.m.

Lucy London, 3rd October 2019

The Wild women's team after their 7-2 win over Sheffield Shadows
(Photo by Paul Breeze)

7 - 2

Our thanks to all the sponsors and to all those who came
To watch the Widnes Wild Women's ice hockey game
At Planet Ice last Sunday versus Sheffield Shadows
The Wild Women deserved a win – goodness only
knows.

Our thanks to the mascot and to the referees –
For that match Ethan Arnold and Josh Humphreys -
Thanks to the bench coaches and the volunteers unseen
And to the Widnes Wild Women's Ice Hockey Team!
And though it is a busy time, we hope you'll all remember
The Wild Women're at home again on the 15th of
December.

Widnes Wild face off against Nottingham Lions (Photo by Paul Breeze)

Well played Widnes Wild - you certainly did us proud
You did your best, fought to the end and roared very,
very loud.
But Nottingham Lions roared louder and just scraped a
goal to win
Widnes Wild your fans are with you, win or lose, through
thick and thin.

Lucy London, 30th September 2019

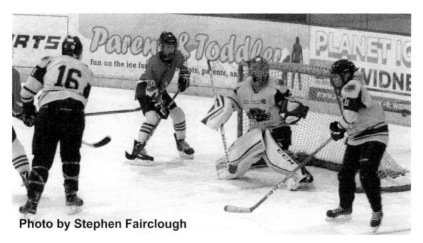
Photo by Stephen Fairclough

The Wild Academy Under 18 team in action (Photo by Steve Fairclough)

Can't get to Altrincham on Saturday? Do not worry -
Don't sit at home fretting and feeling sad and sorry.
Widnes Wild Academy Under 18s Team
Are in action at Planet Ice – they have got to be seen.
Planet Ice Widnes, Face Off 7.45 p.m. Admission free

Lucy London, 3rd October 2019

Photo by David Tattum
DJT Ice Hockey Photos

Blue is the colour of Widnes Wild's warm up strip
And blue is the colour of the logo of Stick
'n' Step, who do so much to help children with Cerebral
Palsy
This season, Stick 'n' Step are The Wild's chosen charity.

Lucy London, 2nd October 2019

Widnes Wild v Solihull Barons in the Midlands Cup (Photo by Geoff White)

3 – 9: Sunday, 13th October 2019

Widnes Wild please don't forget the words of Pierre de Coubertin
Founder of the modern Olympic Games, of which I am a fan:
"The most important thing is to participate"
So listen to Coach Clancy - and remember to concentrate…

Lucy London, 16th October 2019

Wild Academy Under 18 team in action against Deeside (Photo by Stephen Fairclough)

Sunday, 20th October 2019, Planet Ice, Widnes

With ten minutes left on the clock
The Widnes Wild were looking hot
Then Sutton Sting
Went on to win
The Wild could not stop the rot.

Never mind, The Wild Academy Teams are doing well
(We need the youngsters future Wild Teams' ranks to swell).
Well done to Wild Under 15s who continued their winning ways
By winning away at Blackburn – 2 wins in 2 games.

Widnes Wild v Telford Tigers (photo by Hannah Walker)

9 – 1 Widnes Wild v. Telford Tigers 2
17th November 2019

Oh how I enjoyed that game Wonderful Widnes Wild
Under "Fantastic Game" the match report should be filed.
And for all the players, the Coach and Volunteers
And all the staff at Planet Ice in Widnes – three hearty
cheers.

Lucy Poet in Residence, 18.11.2019

Wild v Blackburn Hawks (Photo by Geoff White)

Widnes Wild v Blackburn Hawks 24.XI.2019

The Hawks swooped down on Planet Ice
Thinking a win would be very nice
But the Wild, though seriously depleted
Were not in the mood to be defeated.
A draw it was when full time came
Then the Hawks scored to win the game.
Well played, Widnes Wild – a fantastic match –
You really are a joy to watch.

Lucy Poet in Residence

Widnes Wild 5 Bradford Bulldogs 2

When the Bulldog bites it doesn't let go
But yesterday that was not so
The Wild men won – a joy to see –
As exciting a match as there could be.
WELL DONE
EVERYONE!

Lucy Poet in Residence, 1st December 2019

Widnes Wild 2 Deeside Dragons 4 – 8th December 2019 Planet Ice, Widnes

Dragons came to Widnes all the way from Wales
Complete with fiery breath, wings and silver scales.
A game of three thirds – an-end-to-end fight
A teddy toss to boot – an unforgettable sight.
Could have sworn I saw Santa in the penalty box
But it could have been an illusion – that happens a lot!
The Wild Men fought bravely against their legendary foe
But in the end they couldn't win – oh woe oh woe oh woe.

Lucy Poet in Residence

Sleeping Beauty ice show display at Planet ice Widnes
(Photo by Paul Breeze)

Sleeping Beauty – a Christmas treat
Wonderful costumes and dancing feet
All for you at Planet Ice
Book up now – don't think twice!

Christmas decorations at Planet Ice Widnes (Photo by Paul Breeze)

Planet Ice, Widnes at Christmas 2019

At Planet Ice in Widnes you'll find Santa and his sleigh
Gift-laden like the one he drives on Christmas Day.
But Christmas isn't about presents, turkey and mince pies
We remember the birth of Jesus and visit of 3 kings so
wise
And the star that guided them all those years ago
A symbol of hope for mankind on planet Earth below.

**Lucy Poet in Residence, Planet Ice, Widnes, 24th
November 2019**

Wild netminder Tom McDonald pushes a guest from the Stick n Step charity around the ice in a special "skate with the players" session at Planet Widnes.

(Photo by Dave Smithson)

Lines for Stick 'n' Step on Ice Sunday, 29th December 2019

How wonderful to see Stick 'n' Step on the ice pad
At Widnes Planet Ice – an amazing time was had.
YKK Widnes Wild players helped the children – round
And round the ice they went – a merry sight and sound.
With best wishes to all the YKK Widnes Wild players and
volunteers, Widnes Planet Ice staff and to Stick 'n' Step
personnel, children and families who made this
outstanding event possible. And to my ever-patient and
vigilant Muse.

Lucy Poet in Residence, 31st December 2019

Wild women's pre-match huddle (photo by John Lewis)

While YKK Widnes Wild ice at Deeside away,
Widnes Wild Women's team at home will play.
So lots of ice hockey treats in store
This weekend – to find out more
Check out these websites:
www.widneswild.co.uk / www.icehockeyreview.co.uk

Lucy Poet in Residence

Shannon Holt – Wild women's MVP away at Grimsby (Photo by David Law Photography)

Widnes Wild Women went to Grimsby
Where they won eight to three
And Shannon Holt was M V P.

LL, 12th January 2020

Lines for the Wild Weekend 4th and 5th January 2020

Congratulations Widnes Wild Ice HockeyTeams
Widnes Wild Men, Wild Women and Under Fifteens
You did us proud this past weekend –
Here's hoping that this starts a trend.

Lucy Poet in Residence 7th January 2020

Widnes Wild v Sheffield Senators (photo by Geoff White)

Having defeated Sheffield Senators at Ice Sheffield the day before
Wild's home game on Sunday was hard but never once a bore!
A mountain to climb, a close-run thing, Sunday's game was very tense
Widnes Wild narrowly lost out to a strong Sheffield Senators defence -
In spite of having out-shot the visitors 57 to 37 overall –
The Wild men did their best and can stand very tall.

Lucy Poet in Residence, 13th January 2020

Photo by Hannah Walker

Wild Academy Juniors in an exhibition match (photo by Hannah Walker)

Well done to the Wild Men, Under 15s and Under 13s
Who won their games at the weekend – surpassing all
our dreams
And well played the Under 11s – you lost against one of
the toughest teams.

Lucy Poet in Residence, 22nd January 2020

Sam Anderson playing for the Wild Academy Under 18 team (Photo by Stephen Fairclough)

In A League Of His Own (again...)

Sam Anderson, our hero, Captain and top scorer of Wild
Under 18s
Also ices and scores for several other teams –
The Conference and Widnes Wild - and in the Under 18s
League
He is overall top scorer – what feats for Sam to achieve.

Lucy Poet in Residence, 29th January 2020

Widnes Wild v Bradford Bulldogs (photo by Geoff White)

Well done Widnes Wild for that four-point haul
At the weekend – the Bulldogs to maul.
(For that rhyme I have to thank Paul
Who writes match reports Wild Ones to enthrall.)

Lucy Poet in Residence, 25th February 2020

I could wish for little more
Than for Riverside Raiders to keep score
And my crazy rhymes to write
And weekly match reports to type
And, if I am allowed to choose,
Hugs – when he has time - from my hero Howard
Hughes.

LL 02.02. 2020.

Lines for Widnes Wild Women's match v. Telford Wrekin Raiders 1st March 2020, Planet Ice, Widnes

Yesterday's Wild Women's match was AMAZING –
thanks to everyone who came
And to all of those who contributed to the success of the game
The players in teams Widnes Wild Women and Telford Raiders from Wrekin
Coaches Howard Hughes, Gareth Davies, Charles Humphreys and Michael Parkin
To Ryan Morris, Nicky Jackson and Shannon Holt for their wonderful 50/50 collection
And to everyone else involved – these names are just a selection:
Widnes teams have an amazing fan base – they are all really super.
Thanks to the mascots and to the goal judges Howard Smith and Conor Cooper
Thanks to Julia Shutt and Gary Eddleston for penalty box help and to Andrew Shutt for doing the clock
And to Paul Breeze for announcements and music to make us rock
To Colin Ellis for all his help and for his fantastic game videos
(And of course for Time to go Wild, Colin's amazing radio shows)
To all the staff at Planet Ice in Widnes behind the scenes
And Oh Dear Me, I almost forgot – thanks to the referees.
With sincere apologies to anyone I have left out.

Lucy Poet in Residence, 2nd March 2020

*Match action shots from the Wild women's important wins over Telford –
above - and Grimsby - below (Photos by John Lewis)*

It seems Daniel's Düsseldorfer Eislauf-Gemeinschaft puck and duck
May have brought the Widnes Wild Ice Hockey Team some luck -
Although on Saturday they lost away
On Sunday they won at home – hurray!

Lucy Poet in Residence, 3rd February 2020

Widnes Wild Women v. Grimsby Wolves, Sunday, 16th February 2020

Well done Widnes Wild Women for winning 12 – 2
Oh! How I wish I could have been there watching you
But thanks to Bex Clayton - who does the Wild Men's team Tweets
On Match Days – I was able to keep up with your feats.

Lucy Poet in Residence, 18th February 2020

Paul looking excited at the Laidler Division play off weekend last year – courtesy of Fiona Haggar.

Paul is so excited about the two home matches this weekend that he has been moved to write a poem himself – and here it is:

A double header – what could be better…?
Tigers and Jets – as good as it gets!
A double dose of Widnes Wild
With special offer tickets for adults and child
So don't delay – book today
No need to roam - the YKK-sponsored Wild are at home!

5th March 2020

The Widnes Wild women celebrate a goal (photo by Geoff White)

Lines for Widnes Wild and Wild Women 13th March 2020

Wow! Wow! Widnes Wild - not only a home double header
But 2 wins too – as Paul said in his poem "what could be better"?
This weekend looks likely to be another Wild event
The Women face Sharks, while the Men enter the Dragons' den.

Lucy Poet in Residence, 13th March 2020

Lucy with Pukka the Penguin at a Widnes Wild game, along with some of the toys that feature in her book "The Adventures of Bunny, Archie, Alice & Friends"

(Photos by Paul Breeze)

Lockdown Period 2020/21

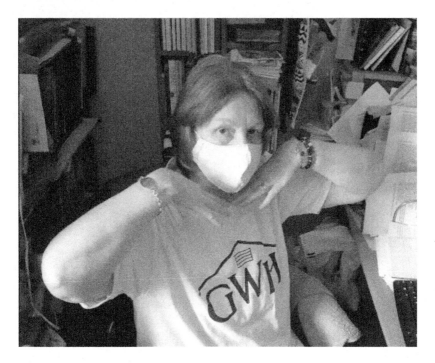

Lockdown Locks

Hope you like my latest look
Took a leaf from Mikey Gilbert's book
With some scissors and a hairband
And a very careful hand
Et voila!

Lucy London, 24th June 2020

It's as much for you as it is for me
If I wear a mask
Beating this Covid thing you see
Is not an easy task.

LL, 22.7.2020

Photo by Paul Breeze
November 2020

Nightmare!

I woke up in the middle of the night -
A nightmare gave me a bit of a fright.
I dreamt I'd forgotten how to keep score
And what the referees' signals were for!

Lucy London, 10th November 2020

Supporting The Wild In Lockdown

Not just a zip – une fermeture éclaire –
More a way of life in everything we wear.
More than just a zip – you assist Wild's winning ways
Thank you YKK – your sponsorship is ace.

Lucy Poet in Residence

WHO'S AWESOME?
You're awesome!

Well done YKK Widnes Wild on winning the North Cup
You really are awesome – just like this pup!
Covid Lockdown challenged you but you all found a way
To keep the team spirit going and keep fit so you could play.
Go Wild!

Lucy Poet in Residence, March 2021

Widnes Wild v Sheffield Scimitars in a behind closed doors Covid series game (photo by Geoff White)

Widnes Wild we love you whether you lose or win
But please try to stay out of that Sin Bin!
Well played Scimitars! I look forward to the match report
And to hearing what everyone else thought.
And I'd be interested to know what all the players think
About playing their matches in an empty rink.
HUGE thanks to everyone today who took part
To the players & coaches, refs and Planet Ice rink staff,
The Wild's amazing volunteers – Drop the Puck*, Colin, Andy and Phil,
Bex, Howard, Andy, Geoff, Nicky, Ailish, Dave, Dick and Gill.
*Gary, Ben, Dave and Peter from BASN

Lucy Poet in Residence, 16h15 Saturday, 20th March 2021

Twitter Queen Bex

Here's Widnes Wild's
Twitter Queen
Bex is her name.

Bex lets us know what's
going on
in every Wild home game.

So when you're on Twitter
during a Widnes Wild
match

Give Bex a wave
and let her know from
whence you watch.

**Lucy Poet in Residence,
25.3.2021**

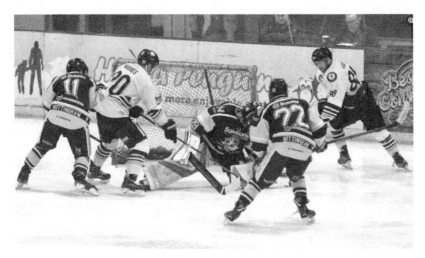

Widnes Wild v Nottingham Lions in a behind closed doors Covid series game (photo by Geoff White)

The Lions roared and then they scored
Widnes Wild replied and equalised
But they couldn't sustain and lost the game.
Better luck next time Widnes Wild.

Lucy Poet in Residence, 10th April 2021

Heads up Wild Ones - the only way is up
You're doing OK in the Three Rivers Cup
It takes time to gel, to play as a team
And it's not that long that together you've been.
Go Wild Ones!

Lucy Poet in Residence, 12.04.2021

Season 2021/22

Ice hockey is coming back!
Widnes Wild on the attack -
Zig zagging round the ice pads -
Widnes Wild the likely lads.

Lucy - Poet in Residence, 2nd July 2021

Hurray Hurray! Here's some Good news today -
Mikey Gilbert, King Ken and Dani Haid
Are all coming back to Widnes Wild to play.
They were part of the team that surely put the Wild
Into Widnes!   Let's go Widnes Wild Ice Hockey Team
Your faithful fans are living the dream.

Lucy - Poet in Residence, 26th June 2021

Another piece of Wild good news
Is the return of our Bez Hughes
(With thanks to my ever-patient Muse…)

Lucy - Poet in Residence, 6th July 2021

Widnes Wild are back on ice – for going to games it's
been a while
The Wild's new fixture list will make Wild Ones smile
But PLEASE take care and protect those you hold dear
Wild Covid advice you will find here:

Lucy - Poet in Residence, September 2021

Widnes Wild are in action this coming weekend
Widnes Wild have a reputation to defend
For Widnes Wild Ice Hockey Team were the proud
winners
Of the prestigious Cups NIHL North and the First Division
On Saturday the Wild face the Blackburn Hawks away
They're at home at Planet Ice to Whitley Warriors on
Sunday.

Lucy - Poet in Residence, 9.9.2021

Not just a zip – une fermeture éclaire –
More a way of life in everything we wear.
More than just a zip – you assist Wild's winning ways
Thank you YKK – your sponsorship is ace.

Lucy - Poet in Residence, October 2021

Why not go along and see
Action from the Wild Academy
Entrance to their matches is free.

Lucy - Poet in Residence, 14.11.2021

Alice sends you all loads of love -
She says it's Wild Women she's thinking of
She hopes you all enjoy the match
And wishes she was there to watch.

Lucy - Poet in Residence, 21.11.2021
*(Alice is the self-appointed mascot of the Widnes Wild
Women's Ice Hockey Team...)*

Well done to one of Wild Academy's Ice Hockey Teams
The Widnes Wild Under Fourteens
For scoring the first competitive goal against Leeds
I'm sure this is the first of many such amazing deeds.

Lucy - Poet in Residence, 23.11.2021

Widnes Wild Ice Hockey Team's Teddy Toss for children
who are ill
In hospital at Christmas Time – a teddy will sweeten the
pill –
At YKK-sponsored Wild home game on 28th November
2021
At Planet Ice in Widnes - you're sure to have lots of fun.

Lucy - Poet in Residence, 23.11.2021

Oh dear me Wild Ones – I've just heard the news -
Covid for Christmas – not something I would choose.
Oh my goodness Wild Ones – what rotten luck -
Covid for Christmas – I'd rather have turkey or duck.
Thinking of you all and sending a healing hug.

Lucy - Poet in Residence, 23rd December 2021

Girls and boys come out to play
Ice hockey – hip hooray!
The Wild Men won away
The Women lost but have upped their game
Win or lose, Wild, we love you just the same.

Lucy - Poet in Residence, 9th February 2022

Shout out to all fans of Widnes Wild:
This is not time to be meek and mild -
It's Time to go Wild! Time to go Wild!
As the Wild are off to the city of Marmalade
Where an important match is to be played.

Lucy - Poet in Residence, 18th February 2022

YKK Widnes Wild face another busy weekend :
On Saturday to Solway Firth their way they wend
On Sunday they play at their home ice rink again
At Planet Ice in Widnes versus Solihull Barons
Play up! Play up! Wonderful Widnes Wild Ones.

Lucy - Poet in Residence, 11 March 2022

On Sunday, 3rd April 2022
Widnes Wild Men are off to face Billingham Stars in the Moralee
Division – that will definitely be an exciting match to see.
Meanwhile, back at the camp, the Wild Women have a match
So if you're at a loose end, why not go along and watch?

Lucy - Poet in Residence, 2.4.2022

Final game of the Moralee Division Season
Sunday 10th April – another good reason
To go and watch Widnes Wild (sponsored by YKK)
As against Sheffield Scimitars they play.

Lucy - Poet in Residence, 8.4.2022

This season's been a roller-coaster ride
For the YKK sponsored Widnes Wild
Today they're away against the Stars of Billingham
(The only rhyme I could find for that is Gillingham…).
On Sunday they host Billingham Stars at Planet Ice
I hope the Wild beat the Stars twice.

Lucy - Poet in Residence, 15.4.2022

Fare you well Rebecca Clayton
known to Wild fans as Bex -
Thank you and good luck
for whatever you do next.

Lucy Poet in Residence, 24 April 2022

Although the season's over there's still lots of Widnes
Wild news
So there are still ice hockey challenges for me and my
muse.
Matty Barlow and Mikey Gilbert have been called to serve
Team
England Under 23 for matches versus Denmark – living
the dream.

Lucy - Poet in Residence, 24th April 2022

Well done Wild Academy Under Tens Ice Hockey Team
You have set the bar very high at a really difficult time
Keep up the good work, continue to B Y B
As through the Wild Age Group Teams you climb.

Lucy - Poet in Residence, May 2022

Here we are at the end of another ice hockey season
And to celebrate Widnes Wild have very good reason.
Finishing third in a higher Division
Is not something to treat with derision.
So get your tickets now for a fabulous celebration –
A buffet, then awards and presentations.

Lucy - Poet in Residence, 12.5.2022

Season 2022/23

Lines for Planet Ice, Widnes

I left a little part
Of my heart, I think
In Widnes Planet Ice Rink,
In the Off Ice Box
Where the clock counts down and the music rocks -
Where I first saw Riverside Raiders Team play -
Wonderful – I'll never forget that day.
That's when we met the life coach Howard
Whose methods our lives have enriched and
empowered.
That's where offending players sit out penalties,
Where volunteers chat to the referees,
Where announcements are made and the score is kept -
At which Gill Gillingham is the most adept -
Where Shannon Holt, Mike Rogers and Josh Humphreys
we met
Where Sam Anderson showed me how to work The
Clock -
I think I remember how to start it and stop...
Where Dick Gillingham looks after every puck -
At Planet Ice nothing is left to luck -
Where ice hockey fans come for information,
And where I always got amazing inspiration.

Lucy Poet in Residence, 4 September 2022

At Planet Ice in Widnes
In the run up to Christmas
You can see an ice show

117

With characters you will surely know –
Ebenezer Scrooge and Marley.
Tickets are selling fast and there are hardly
Any left! So hurry and book via the website
As its going to be a wonderful night.

Lucy Poet in Residence 7th Nov 2022

Wishing a Very Happy Christmas to ALL Widnes Wild Ice
HockeyTeams –
Players, coaches, managers, fans and every volunteer –
May Santa fill your stockings with the gifts of your
dreams.
Here's to a safe, healthy, happy and prosperous New
Year.

Lucy Poet in Residence, 23.12.2022

Zip fasteners are made by the wonderful firm YKK
Who sponsor Widnes Wild ice hockey team home and away
As the team zip and zig zag around the ice pad -
Follow this link to see the season they've had:
https://www.widneswild.co.uk/news

28th January 2023

Widnes Wild women's players Katie Fairclough, Ellie Green and Ellen Tyrer model the new DMUK sponsored home shirts (Photo by Paul Breeze)

Thank you to the company DMUK
Who are sponsoring Wild Women's shirts home and away
They are launching the shirts during the match today.

Lucy Poet in Residence, 5 February 2023

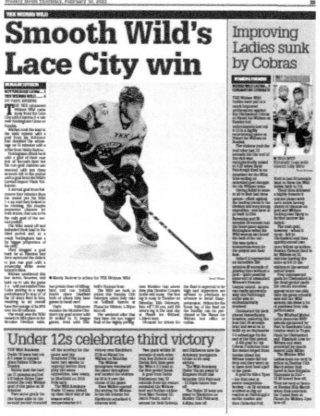

Smooth Wild's Lace City win

Improving Ladies sunk by Cobras

Under 12s celebrate third victory

Widnes Weekly News 10th February 2022, Page 29

Girls and boys come out to play
Ice hockey – hip hooray!
The Wild Men won away
The Women lost but have upped their game
Win or lose, Wild, we love you just the same.

Lucy Poet in Residence, 9th February 2022

In A League Of His Own (Mk III)

Sam Anderson, our hero, former Captain and top scorer
of the Under 18s
Also iced and scored for several other teams –
The Conference and Widnes Wild and in the Under 18s
League
He was overall top scorer – what feats for Sam to
achieve.
And now he is an Ice Hockey referee.
Happy Birthday, Sam.

Lucy Poet in Residence, 11 February 2023

Play Off Quarter Final - Wild V Barons

Saturday 1st April – Moralee Play Off Quarter Final,

Match Report: Diamonds 1 - Wild Women 12

Sunday 2nd April – WNIHL Div 2 N Kingston

Too many Wild men on the ice, alas, alack
But three Wild women scored hatricks
I'm sure the Wild Men, like the phoenix from the flame,
Will arise and find their winning streak again.

LL, 3.4.2023

10 Years In The Wild

Widnes Wild
Ice Hockey Team
Doing their best always
Never disappointing
Every match exciting
Skating like lightning.

Widnes Wild
Ice Hockey Team
Long may you continue
Delighting.

HAPPY TENTH ANNIVERSARY WILD ONES!

Lucy Poet in Residence, 20th March 2023

*Adam Wrixon in action for the North West Lions at the Czech tournament
(Photo by Jiri Bosek)*

Lines for the North West Lions

The North West Lions Ice Hockey Team
To the Czech Republic have recently been
To take part in an International Tournament
Rather a lot of penalties meant
The pride of the Lions got a bit of a dent.
But Lions, don't forget the words of Pierre de Coubertin
Founder of the modern Olympic Games, of which I am a
fan,
"The most important thing Is not to win
But to participate"
So, listen to your Coach and concentrate…

Lucy Poet in Residence, 7th April 2023

The Wild Academy Under 12 team celebrate winning the league title
(photo by Hannah Walker)

Lines for the Widnes Wild U12 Ice Hockey Team on winning the EIHA North U12 League title, April 2023

Well done Widnes Wild Under Twelves
You have really excelled yourselves
Stars of the future
We salute you
Congratulations!

Lucy - Poet in Residence, 12th April 2023

The Widnes Under 16 team receive their runners up medals at Sheffield
(Photo by MyTeamPhoto)

Lines for Wild Academy Under 16s July 2023

Wild Academy Under 16
Ice Hockey Team -
Runners up at Sheffield Tournament,
Recently - which meant
Overall they came second
Which is fantastic I reckon.

Lucy Poet in Residence, 19th July 2023.

SUMMER 2023

Halton Huskies team photo 2023 (Photo by @haganovaphoto)

Halton Huskies

Rec. Ice Hockey Team Halton Huskies
Play their home games in Widnes
Ice Rink – Planet Ice,
Where, for a reasonable price,
You can watch them play
Every home match day

Lucy London, 2023, 17th May.

Connah's Quay Cobras team photo, April 2023 (Photo by Sophie Harrison Jones / HJ Photography)

Connah's Quay Cobras

I knew about Deeside Dragons Ice Hockey Team and have often seen them play
But I didn't find out about the Deeside-based Team Connahs Quay Cobras till today…

LL, 2023 – 19 May

Raiders player Ben Donkin with his cuddly alter-ego
mascot "Ben Dogkin" (Photo by Paul Breeze)

Saturday 10th June – Summer Classic Cup
Riverside Raiders 9 – Blackburn Buccaneers 5

Put out more flags and ring those bells
For this is what my story tells
The Riverside Raiders are back
Onto their winning track!

Lucy Poet in Residence, 11 June 2023

The Manchester Mayhem sledge team with sponsors from the Fletcher Group solicitors (photo by @haganovaphoto)

Manchester Mayhem hit the headlines again.

After giving Peterborough Phantoms a great game.
Mayhem are setting out today
To play Peterborough Phantoms away.
Tip off is at four p. m.
Don't miss out watch Manchester Mayhem.

LL 24.6.2023

*Cuddly mascot Mayhem Markus at a sledge game at Widnes
(Photo by Paul Breeze)*

Mayhem Markus

Mayhem remember the ethic of Pierre de Coubertin,
Founder of the modern Olympic Games of which I am a
fan,
It's more important to participate than to win
Taking part is the most important thing.

With a number of key players missing
This season has been a period of transition
Never mind the team's final BPIHL Table position.
Mayhem Markus hopes he is a welcome addition…

Lucy Poet in Residence, 17th July 2023

The Riverside Raiders celebrate winning the Summer Classic Cup Play Offs to add to their 2023 Conference and League titles

R IVERSIDE
A lways entertain us
I cing
D ucking and diving
E xciting
R iverside Raiders
S uper League Champs and Heroes

H USKIES
A lthough you didn't win
L ook to the future
T eam Halton Huskies
O nwards
N ever give in.

Congratulations!

Lucy Poet in Residence, 8th August 2023

Lucy with referees Stephen French and Ray Ormes at a Wild women's match at Widnes in December 2018 (Photo by Paul Breeze)

Lucy and Her "French & Ormes" Poem
The full story – by Paul Breeze

Lucy - as you may know - is one of the world authorities on World War One and its poetry. Yes - it's true. She has a worldwide network of contacts and even gets University professors asking her things and, while I am a mere minnow in the lake of poetry and literary understanding by comparison, we do agree on one thing.

We both absolutely hate it when so called experts give their opinion on something that somebody else has written.

What I mean here is when some modern day authority looks back at, say, a piece of war poetry that a soldier wrote in a trench over 100 years ago and says very self-importantly "of course, what he is referring to here is...." where in the most part, that it is purely THEIR INTERPRETATION and not based on any particular fact or knowledge at all. It is - essentially – just what they "would have thought..."

They can't possibly have a direct line into the head of somebody else and can't possibly know what they were thinking of or necessarily going through at the time that they wrote any particular poem.

If you happened to have a diary entry or a letter from, say Wilfred Owen or Siegfried Sassoon, where they specifically say:

"Had nice relaxing walk in the woods today – wrote a poem about squirrels..."

then you could possibly argue that you know the circumstances to their poem "Squirrels In The Woods".

However, in most cases, we don't have access to this sort of qualifying information, so people can only speculate – which isn't particularly ideal.

Despite not being a huge fan of poetry as such – although I am interested in the lives of the poets – I actually arrived at a similar conclusion myself several years before I even met Lucy and ages before we had started on producing her exhibitions and books.

I was studying a module on French Literature at University in the mid 90s and we were doing poems by Apollinaire.

Now, our lecturer at the time – who was, by the way, very good – I won't name her but she is, in fact, now a world famous novelist who is described on Amazon and

Wikipedia and so on as a "Sunday Times bestseller" and a "New York Times bestseller" - so obviously trying teach me French literature must have put her off academia for life....

Anyway, she said something about one of the poems we were reading that I didn't agree with. It was talking about a stream streaming downhill and the text contained lots of S sounds and she said that the poet was "OBVIOUSLY referring to the sounds of the stream" with all these S's in the verses.

While I acknowledge that it was quite a clever conclusion to arrive at, I did think at the time that the back-story to this poem could just as easily be something completely different.

He could just as easily have been sitting outside a Parisian cafe surrounded by hustle and bustle, half pissed and completely stressed as he had to write a poem in a rush to complete an important commission – and he just wrote any old thing that came into his head.

To my mind, both scenarios are completely valid and, just because she had a PhD in French Literature and I was at the time editing a fanzine on German football, without any supporting evidence one way or the other, there is nothing to suggest that she was any more correct than I was.

I didn't argue this point at the time, by the way – although I do know that Academics love that sort of round and round pointless theorising discussion – but the was another interesting thing that came out of the literature module as well.

She said she found it impossible to mark a particular essay that I had written about one of the books that we were studying ("Le Blé en Herbe" by Colette) because it came across "more like a piece of post-graduate research work than a first year degree assignment" (paraphrased – but near enough...).

She didn't know what to do with it so just gave it the middle mark so as to have something to put down in my results. I never really knew what she meant by that - but have always looked upon it as some sort of compliment.

Interestingly enough – admittedly going further off the point somewhat – in first year degree-level German, I once got an A+ for a translation assignment. This was in the days before the infamous boom of "grade inflation" and it was practically impossible to get an A+ for things.

In fact, I think it was the first time in donkey's years that anybody had got an A+ for anything in German and the lecturing staff actually went so far as to ask my permission to keep it and use it as an example to show other students how a good translation should be done.

I was also once asked (and - indeed - paid, would you believe ...) to give a talk to final year students about how a dissertation should be laid out – but I think that was due to the fact that I was the only person they could find hanging around in the corridor at the time who was free to do it, to be honest...

And don't get me started on the day's teaching experience that I had at Little Lever School in Bolton. I've got a certificate for that somewhere.

Anyway, you'll be pleased to know that this is eventually leading up to an ice hockey related topic.

Just on the off chance that anybody might be wanting to study the Poetry of Lucy London in 100 years time – be it in schools or universities (if they still have them then), I am going to provide you with a first-hand completely authentic account of how a particular poem came to be written and the full story behind it.

Therefore, there will be no need by the academics of the future to speculate as to what she was thinking about at the time that she wrote this particular poem and what or who it was about. It is all about to be immortalised in black and white – by me, who was there.

When Lucy was at University in Preston, one of her French lecturers was called Mark Orme. She has kept in contact with him since graduating and they often exchange messages via Facebook and elsewhere.

On one such occasion, Mark mentioned to Lucy that the name Orme was of French origin and that he himself had French grandparents. The word "orme" means elm tree in French and that is where the town of Ormskirk in west Lancashire originally got its name.

Shortly after hearing this, Lucy and I were helping at a Riverside Raiders game at Planet Ice Widnes and it turned out that Ray Ormes was the referee (you can see where we are heading here – can't you...?).

Knowing that orme meant elm tree in French and that was where the town of Ormskirk got its name and that Mark Orme had French grandparents, Lucy asked Ray "Excuse me, but is your name French?"

He looked slightly puzzled by this – particularly as he had his name clearly emblazoned across his back - and replied politely "Erm, No it's Ormes. Ray Ormes."

They both looked slightly perplexedly at each other and then Ray skated off to do something referee-like out on the ice

Now, I thought that this was absolutely hilarious – crossed purposes at its very best. I fully understood why Lucy had asked the question that she had asked - but Ray, having had the potential French-ness of his origins suddenly thrown at him in the middle of an ice hockey match, was not fully up to speed.

In fact – he obviously thought that Lucy had confused him with a completely different ice hockey referee called Stephen French (who I already knew but she didn't...) and he clearly sought to correct her in this matter.

After I had got up off the floor and recovered from my roaring with laughter at this misunderstanding and the consternation that it had appeared to have caused to both parties, I explained all this to Lucy and she saw the funny side of it as well.

Later on, after the game, we sent a message to Ray and explained it all to him as well and he also thought it very funny.

Some months later, we were helping at a Wild women's team's league game and I rushed into our office at the rink (OK – it doubles occasionally as the First Aid Room as well...) in a state of great excitement. It took me a while to get my breath and even then I could only just manage to utter the words:

"French and Ormes...!"

"What do you mean?" came the reply from Lucy who was mid-way through putting all her layers on... (that's warm clothing, by the way - not make up...)

"French and Ormes!" I said again with a bit more oomph - pointing frantically towards the referees' changing room that was next door... and the message was finally got across. Stephen French and Ray Ormes were the two referees for the game.

So we all had a bit of a laugh about the previous matter of confusion and I got them to pose with Lucy for a photo afterwards to go with her resulting poem.

And, there you are. If you ever, in the years to come, hear somebody blindly theorising about the meaning of the French & Ormes poem by Lucy London, you can now give them chapter and verse on the whole thing!

And the whole story is now set out in full for the benefit of future generations of scholars and academics - like my now world famous French literature lecturer.

And also the story behind my photo - if it comes to it...

French and Ormes

"Is your name french?" I asked Mr Ormes,
Thinking of the origin rather than the form.
"No, it's Ormes", Mr Ormes replied –
My husband laughed until he cried.
You see, what I did not know then
There's a ref. called French – beyond my ken.
On Sunday both reffed at Planet Ice
So Paul took this photo - which is very nice!
Thanks guys!

Lucy London, 10th December 2018

Lucy's Songwriting

May 2019:

The Widnes Wild women's team will be cheered onto the ice with a brand new song that has been especially written for them when they play the last home game in their turbulent WPL season this Sunday 19th May against the Sheffield Shadows at Planet Ice Widnes – 5.30pm face off.

The song – entitled "The Girls…!" - has been written by the Wild's Poet In Residence Lucy London who has been a keen follower of women's sports for many years and has been particularly impressed by the attitude of the struggling Wild women's team this season.

The women's team have lost all of their league games to date after losing a large number of long-standing players during the summer and taking on a whole new squad of inexperienced players in a bold experiment in team building to help secure the club's longer term future.

Talking about how the song came about, Lucy said:

"I am always coming up with ideas, jotting down lines for poems and songs and I like to write things to support the various ice hockey teams at Widnes."

"At a recent women's team match, somebody from the visiting team expressed surprise that we were putting so much effort into the game day experience as it was "only women…". "

"I immediately put him straight and told him that we don't differentiate at Widnes and that we try and put on the same show, it be men's games, women's games, junior games or rec games. However, it still irked me for a few days afterwards and in the end, I came up with the words to a song to celebrate women's involvement in sport."

Determined that the song should be a rousing anthem to help cheer the Wild women on, Lucy contacted Canadian musician friends Jason Moon and Jaime April – originally from Prince Albert, Saskatchewan, but now residing in Liverpool - to help out with the tune.

Jason and Jaime came up with a superb rousing tune to go with the lyrics and also produced a professional recording of the song to be played at the Wild Women's team's future home games at Planet Ice Widnes.

You can hear the song at the Wild women's game on Sunday – face off 5.30pm - or, if you can't wait that long, you can also listen to it now on Soundcloud by clicking on the link below.

Jason and Jaime also play in the bands April Moon and Wooden Rocket and can regularly be seen playing live around the North West and beyond.

The Girls...!

The boys! The boys! They may be back in town
But the girls haven't exactly been waiting around!
When there's stuff to be done, the girls don't shirk
They get their sleeves rolled up and get to work

Chorus
The girls! The girls! The girls are here to stay
The girls! The girls who haven't been away
You can count on us to get things done
Come on girls let's have some fun.

Just because we're girls shouldn't mean we get left out
Life is for living – that's what it's all about.
We can climb mountains and play football too
And cricket and ice hockey – just like the boys do.

Chorus

The girls! The Girls! Don't dismiss us as "only"
Without us the world would be very lonely.
We're the girls, the girls don't push us away
We're the girls, the girls and we're here to stay.

Chorus x 3 to fade....

Lyrics by Lucy London © Copyright 2019
Music by Jason Moon and Jaime April
Musical Notation by Richard Lawrence
Music Publishing by Posh Up North Publishing

Lucy presenting Howard Hughes with a CD copy of the song that she wrote for the Riverside Raiders team. (Photo by Paul Breeze)

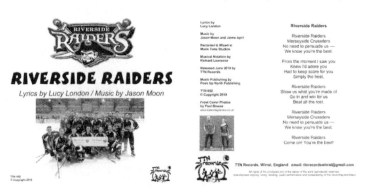

Riverside Raiders

Riverside Raiders
Merseyside Crusaders
No need to persuade us –
We know you're the best.
From the moment I saw you
Knew I'd adore you
Had to keep score for you
Simply the best.
Riverside Raiders
Show us what you're made of
Go in and win for us
Beat all the rest.
Riverside Raiders
Merseyside Crusaders
No need to persuade us –
We know you're the best.
Riverside Raiders
Come on! You're the best!

Lucy London, 22nd May 2019

Lyrics by Lucy London © Copyright 2019
Music by Jason Moon
Musical Notation by Richard Lawrence
Music Publishing by Posh Up North Publishing

Widnes Wild Song (in search of music...)

Are you ready for a slide on the Wild side? (This can be spoken…)

Planet Ice in Widnes Town's
Where Widnes Wild play – come on down
Come and join the happy throng
Of Wild fans as they sing this song.
Are you read for a slide on the Wild side -
Are you ready to have some fun?
Time to go Wild in Widnes, zig zag Wild Ones!

Chorus:

Widnes Wild, Widnes Wild – such a wild child -
Ever since you began back as Fylde Flyers.
Widnes Wild, Widnes Wild winning every cup
Carry on your winning ways – the only way is up.
For all the Wild players, coaches and volunteers
And all the staff at Planet Ice – lets have a cheer.

Like the phoenix rising from the flame
The Wild rise again and again
Widnes Wild guys are very tough
Never say die and never give up.

Chorus:

Widnes Wild, Widnes Wild – such a wild child -

Ever since you began back as Fylde Flyers.
Widnes Wild, Widnes Wild winning every cup
Carry on your winning ways – the only way is up.
For all the Wild players, coaches and volunteers
And all the staff at Planet Ice – lets have a cheer.

Widnes Wild Academy Teams too
Everyone looks to you
Making us proud – let's hear it loud
For all those Wild Teams do.

Chorus:

Widnes Wild, Widnes Wild – such a wild child -
Ever since you began back as Fylde Flyers.
Widnes Wild, Widnes Wild winning every cup
Carry on your winning ways – the only way is up.
For all the Wild players, coaches and volunteers
And all the staff at Planet Ice – let's have a cheer.

Lyrics © Lucy London, May 2021

Paul with Kingston Diamonds player – and excellent photographer - Lois Tomlinson (Photo by Geoff White)

Above left: Paul presenting the highly contentious box of chocolates as an MVP award to Wild's Sav Sumner (Photo by Geoff White) Above right: PB in typical multi-tasking mode at a women's game – announcing the MVPs from the middle of the ice so as to be able to take the photos as well. (Photo by Andrew Shutt)

EIHA Women's Premier League
Sunday 21st February 2016

Widnes Wild Women 1 – Milton Keynes Falcons 2
Period Scores: (0-2, 1-0, 0-0)
Shots on Goal: Widnes 41 – MK 22
Penalties: Widnes 20 – MK 4
Widnes Scoring: Leen De Decker 1+0

The Widnes Wild ladies team put on a battling display in their first home game of the season but ended up losing 1-2 to the Milton Keynes Falcons.

www.icehockeyreview.co.uk

Paul & Lucy And Sponsoring The Wild Women's MVP Awards

I (me - Paul here...) have always been a keen follower of women's ice hockey, going all the way back to the early 1980s when my local Peterborough Ravens team won the first modern day English league title.

One of the Ravens players was in my year at school and another lived a few doors down my road. In later years a couple of them played on the same rec team that I did and I actually bought a secondhand pair of playing shorts off Kim Strongman – before she went on to be a Queen Bee Elite player and long standing GB international!

So when we found out that Widnes was going to have a women's team, Lucy and I jumped at the chance to go along and support them.

As women's hockey never gets as much attention as the men's games, I started off writing match reports for all their games. The home games were easier as we went to all of those and I then started closely studying the gamesheets for the away games and putting together reports for those as well.

The Wild women played their first home game in the early months of 2016 and the game lacked a bit of atmosphere because there wasn't initially any music or announcing. Having originally decided to have a year off, I did think about offering my services but, by the time I got round my shyness, Patrick Sinclair had started doing the match calling using the rink's radio microphone so I decided to forget about it.

We had been in contact with original team captain Charlene Chapman about sponsoring something or other, albeit without really getting very far and, at the penultimate home game against Whitley Bay Squaws on 8th May, I suddenly took it upon myself to march in to the officials' booth and announced that Charlene had said that Lucy could present the MVP awards.

She HAD touched upon it vaguely in a previous email but certainly nothing had been formally agreed so I wasn't really sure how this overture would go down.

The lady doing everything in the box peered at me over her glasses in a very severe "and who the hell are you...?" sort of manner and then, indeed, did ask me who I was.

Slipping into safety default mode, I replied: "Paul & Lucy", somewhat oblivious to the fact that any casual onlooker might think this rather odd as I was standing there on my own at the time.

However, it is worth bearing in mind that being "Paul & Lucy" used to open a lot of doors in Blackpool and the surrounding area when we were doing our radio shows and our Best Kept Secrets website - and it also had the desired effect here as she realised that it was us who had been writing the match reports for the women's games.

She introduced herself as Mandy Sinclair – mother of the player Sophie Sinclair–Reeks - and said how much they all appreciated the work we had been doing on their behalf.

So, by the end of the game, I finally got round to telling Lucy that she was going to present the MVP awards. I left it until the last moment on purpose so that she didn't have time to get nervous about it and think of all sorts of reasons why she couldn't possibly do it – and around we went.

There was no photographer that day so I bravely ventured out onto the ice and took the presentation photos.

8th May 2016: Lucy presents the MVP award to Amy Moran of Whitley Bay Squaws (Photo by Paul Breeze)

The 15th January 2017 is another important date in this story as the Wild women were due to play Streatham Storm in the WPL at Widnes.

Through having written a story for the Wild website and the newspaper about Sophie having been selected to play for the Team GB Under 18 women's international team in Poland, I had picked up on the fact that Mandy and Patrick were going out to watch her and they were not going to be at the Streatham game.

I pointed this out to the women's team and, having just successfully broken my announcing duck at Widnes by doing the Widnes Wildcats v Riverside Raiders Antony Morris memorial game the week before, I offered to step in and help out.

The run up to this game was a bit bizarre as the Manchester Phoenix team had been given permission to play the rest of their EPL games for the season at Widnes, rather than dragging their long suffering fans all the way to Blackpool to use the rather dubious Fylde Coast Ice Arena. The first of these games took place on the same day as the Wild women v Streatham match and the women's game was moved to an earlier face off time to accommodate it.

The Women's team were up in arms about this late change as several of their players had got their work shifts arranged around a 5.30 pm face off and couldn' t change them that easily – and the head coach at the time also went ballistic and provided me with few choice comments that I could never get away with printing anywhere!

The face off was supposed to be at 4pm so Lucy and I arrived at 3pm to get set up only to find that the skating session was still very much underway and not actually due to finish until 4pm.

There was a heightened air of tension around the place as nobody really knew what was going to happen with the Phoenix game – how many people would turn up and how it would all go. The rink manager Kirsty was prowling up and down and there was also another manager chappy who I didn't know and have never seen before or since who was also there helping to keep on top of things.

We got set up and managed to get soundchecked once the disco music had finished - and Joanne Gibson from Bradford came along and did the EGS for the game.

It was a very close and entertaining game and Streatham just won 2-3 with a late goal. You can watch Colin's highlights compilation on YouTube and one of the fascinating points about this game isn't so much the game at all but all of the people who kept wandering in and out of the rink as it went on.

The Phoenix game was due to start at 6.30 and all of their fans arrived in plenty of time. As it was free admission to the women's game, they all came into the rink and sat down or milled about in the walkways. So at the start of the video, there is hardly anyone there – as it was an odd face off time – and then by the end the place is absolutely heaving with all these Phoenix fans.

They were also planning to do a livestream of the game for fans who couldn't get to Widnes to watch and this was a big money earner for the hard up Phoenix team. It was important for them to get it working right and they had a huge amount of equipment to bring in and set up beforehand.

So, throughout the women's game, during which yours truly was trying to concentrate on playing the music and getting the announcements right (this was, after all, the first senior league game that I had ever worked on), a procession of Phoenix people kept coming along asking where they could set things up and plug things in.

Then the girl who was going to do the music for the Phoenix game came in and asked about linking up to the sound system. She also asked me rather enigmatically if anybody had spoken to me about announcing for their game – which they hadn't – and nobody ever did, so I don't really know what that was all about.

Then Neil Morris came along (you either know who he is or you don't - check out Stuart Latham's book about Manchester Phoenix to find out more about him...) and he also poked around and looked at the sockets for the sound cables and then asked me if I knew anywhere locally where you could buy audio leads. At 5pm on a Sunday ....!

Needless to say, I politely replied in the negative while trying to carry on keeping up with the game that I was actually there for.

Now, what actually surprised me about all of this is that you have a team playing in the EPL - ie two divisions above Widnes Wild – being run by people who, apparently, organise huge international live events but, for some reason, nobody had thought to drop into the rink during the week before the game to check out the lie of the land, where the sockets were and what sort of leads they might need to bring with them....

But there you go. After the trials and tribulations of the women's game and the additional hassle of having to

154

deal with all sorts of odd people and their random enquiries, we scuttled off to go and have a well earned McDonalds and left them all to it....

25th February 2018: The Match In Question...

On this particular day, I had arranged to meet up with the Kingston Diamonds player Lois Tomlinson after the game and give her a copy of my NIHL Yearbook because she had kindly provided me with some photos to use in it earlier in the season. As Geoff White the official Wild photographer was going to be there, we decided to make it part of the after match presentations and give it a bit of extra attention.

When I arrived, I went into the officials booth and told Mandy what I wanted to do at the end of the game and she said "OK – you might as well present the MVP awards as well, in that case."

During one of the breaks, Geoff came up to me and said that Mandy had told him that I was presenting the MVP awards. He explained that he always had trouble getting the women's players to stand still long enough after they had been given the award to be able to take a decent photo and asked if I could try and do something about this for the presentation – so I gave it a bit of thought.

Now, I have to say that the presentation on the ice after this particular game was a thoroughly life changing experience – in a nice way, that is – more than I ever could possibly have imagined - and I learnt a huge amount of lessons as a consequence of it.

The first thing that you need to know is - if you have ever been on the ice – or stood at the door of the penalty box at the end of a game - it is a really thrilling experience, with the crowd cheering and the players skating round and shaking hands and the music blaring and the bustling activity behind the scenes.

In fact, the first time that I ever did this (in the "modern era"...) - when I presented the MVP awards at the Wild v Hull Jets men's game in March 2016, it took me a week to come down afterwards and the whole thing remains a sort of haze to this day.

The other thing that you won't know if you haven't been out on the ice is how the plexi glass affects the acoustics around the rink. If you are off the ice and somebody on the other side of the glass tries to talk to you, you can't hear what they say and you have to go to an opening in order to be able to communicate.

This means that you don't too hear much of what goes on between the players on the ice nor what the referee says to them.

When I first started watching ice hockey at Peterborough in the 1980s, there was no plexi glass at the rink - just netting that hung around the boards.

However, this meant that you could hear the interaction among the players and you could also clearly hear the referee's instructions. When the play was stuck against the board, you'd hear the ref shouting out "Play It ! Play It!" or you'd hear the linesman shouting "No Icing!" when he waved off a call after an end to end shot had clipped somebody on the way past.

And, when the referee blew to give a penalty – you could clearly hear him call out, for example   "Number 2 White. Two minutes for cross checking " or whatever the call was for....

Now, knowing for a fact that this used to happen in the old days, when I became an off ice game official at games at Widnes and was involved with the announcing , occasionally scoring and keeping an eye on the scoreboard and penalty boxes, I was constantly surprised when a player would come into the penalty box, flop onto the bench, throw his gear on the floor and exclaiming "What was that for...?".

I would then have to spend half the game patiently explaining to the various players what penalties they had been given and how long they would be sitting in the box.

I eventually asked one of the referees at a game one day if they still called out what the penalty was for when they blew the whistle out on the ice as I was rather surprised that the players never seemed to know what they had been penalised for.

He explained that usually, when the whistle got blown, the players would be all up in arms either pushing and shoving the opposition or arguing about the call with the officials - and would then whinge and complain all the way to the penalty box, which is why they never knew what the penalty had been called for.

Anyway, back to the end of February 2018 and I went round to the officials bench at the end of the game to make the presentations. On my way onto the ice, a small box of chocolates was pressed into my hand to give as the MVP award and I stood there awaiting the verdict.

There was no music on this occasion – and only a fairly small crowd – so it was rather eerie and quiet out on the ice compared to usual and you could clearly hear all the whispers between the players on both sides.

At this time we were using the box nearer to the away team so I was right in the firing line in terms of comments from their players - and they were moaning and complaining in my direction about something or other.

I think they were criticising the fact that the MVP award was a piffling box of chocolates rather than a trophy that they might usually have expected to receive. This was actually nothing to do with me as I had just had it sprung on me at the last minute so there wasn't much I could do about it.

There wasn't any microphone on the go for this game either - for some reason – and being the only one who could be audible across the ice because of my positioning I ended up having to call out the winners of the awards as well.

Presumably, from the players' point of views, this made it look as if I had actually selected them, which I can guarantee you I did not - and, indeed, never have - because I would have trouble selecting an MVP even if there was only one player on the ice!

I touched on this earlier but it is worth explaining in full at this point so that you understand what I just said. It is true that, as a match announcer or scorer or whatever, you have a front row seat and often sit about 6 inches from the action of the game. But the very nature of the job – where you have to write everything down and get it properly entered on the game sheet – means that you don't always have the luxury of being able to watch / enjoy the game.

In fact, I probably spend as much time looking at the clock for how long is left until the next announcement is needed – or how long a penalty has left to run – or at the penalty box to make sure the right players are there and who is going out next etc – or where the person is with the results of the raffle that is due to be called out at the next period break – as I do actually watching the game.

So it was called out to me who the winner of the MVP award was for the Hull team (the away team always goes first) – and I in turn called this out across the ice.

It was Sophie Campbell who had scored 3+1 in the game and the game had finished 1-5 to the Kingston Diamonds - so it wasn't an unreasonable call and one I might even have arrived at myself based on a quick look at the scoring figures on the gamesheet.

But the Hull girls were in full swing by this point and this announcement was received with a torrent of maybe not abuse, but certainly some rather sarcastic catcalls.

As Campbell came over to collect her box of chocolates, I enacted my masterplan to help the photographer get a decent MVP photo for once.

As she approached, I asked her to take her helmet off for the photo. Luckily she was quite young and little and just did what I asked – probably in shock – and we got a nice posed photo taken.

She put her gloves and stick down on the ice so that she could undo her helmet and then took that off and laid it on the ice as well. My strategy was working quite well and after all that fuss and upheaval, she stood completely still, smiling sweetly for the shot.

Had it been one of the other more vociferous players, I am not sure if it would have gone quite so well.

Then it was time for the Widnes MVP award winner to be announced. I looked up and saw all these eyes piercing burning into me from behind the masks lined up along the other blue line.

At the time, I imagined that they were all looking at me hopefully, imploringly, desperately wishing to be called out as the MVP but I came to realise later that they were probably hoping that it wasn't them - and that there was no way they were going to take THEIR helmet off for a photo and box of chocolates.

But I was also in full swing by now and, in aloof "Important Person" mode, I ignored the crescendos of chuntering that were building up from both sets of players and I called out Sammi Boyle from the Wild women and got her to take her helmet off for the photo as well.

Then I called over Lois Tomlinson from the Hull team and that really set the cat among the proverbial pigeons as only she, me and Geoff knew about this one and there were surprised shouts of "Eh? What's this for...?" and so on....

So – mission accomplished. All awards presented – all photos safely taken, along with a great publicity shot for my book – and I went for a bit of a lie down!

I suggested to Patrick Sinclair that I actually had my sound equipment in the car as Lucy and I were doing the Halton Huskies game later that same evening and had we known in advance, I could have brought it in earlier for the women's game.

The final Wild women's home game of the season was scheduled for a few weeks later – against Bracknell Firebees, and once again we were due to do a Huskies game the same day - so we arranged to do that and I did the music and Patrick did the announcing.

We did the same thing again taking the helmets off for the photos but this time we used the side closer to the Widnes blueline - and to be - honest the away players were less belligerent on this occasion.

The MVP winners were Claire Fay for Bracknell (Daniel Fay's mum...) and Sav Sumner for Widnes – who did moan a bit about probably having "helmet hair"...

We don't bother with the taking off of the helmets any more – for the following season Lucy devised an ever better strategy for getting the MVP photos done - and there are several very good reason for this:

1) It makes everybody HATE you

2) They got used to the idea of MVP photos and didn't skate off as quickly afterwards

3) There is a chance that the award winner might be under 18 and under 18s are not allowed to remove their helmets on the ice at any time – so best to be on the safe side

During the summer months, I was looking back at the photos we had taken during the course of the season and in a Damask flash of inspiration (yes – I was at the dining table), I suddenly understood what the Hull players had been whining on about.

At the end of a men's game, each team usually gets presented with a crate of beer – with enough bottles or cans for one for each player. Fair enough.

At most women's games they get a little statuette of some sort – but here was some bloke giving out little boxes of chocolates that didn't even have enough in them for one each among the players.

It seemed a little condescending and, in hindsight, I could fully appreciate why they were a bit miffed about it.

That's not to say that I was criticising whoever had kindly provided the chocolates as it meant that there were at least prizes to give out and even 12 little boxes of choccies over the course of the season still costs money after all...

I pointed this out to Lucy and suggested the WE could sponsor the MVP awards for the next season. We could do it in the name of one of the First World War women that she was researching and it would be good publicity all round.

The Women's team were pleased with the idea as it removed a cost and an extra task for them to worry about for the next season and that is how it all came about.

Shannon Holt displays the Sarah MacNaughtan Memorial MVP award for the 2018/29 Wild Women's season (Photo by Paul Breeze).

Sarah MacNaughtan Memorial Award
Widnes Wild Women's Ice Hockey Team MVP Awards
WPL Season 2018/19

https://sarahmacnaughtanmemorialaward.blogspot.com/

December 2018: There will be a new name on the MVP awards for the Widnes Wild women's team's home games this season and, rather than being one of the players, it will be the name of a World War One Heroine!

The Wild's Poet In Residence Lucy London is sponsoring the match awards and is using the opportunity to spread the word about Sarah MacNaughtan – who was quite well known prior to the First World War but is all but forgotten today.

Lucy explains the story behind this:

"Since 2012, I've been researching the role of women in the First World War for a series of commemorative exhibitions. Having commemorated the First World War all my life it was not until I began researching for this project that I began to discover what women accomplished before they were allowed to vote. Women served in many of the theatres of the conflict and many of them died or were killed.

Yet there are many of those women whose names do not appear on the Commonwealth War Graves Commission List of Female Casualties and, I have just found out that some of them may not even have graves, let alone a mention on a war memorial.

Sarah MacNaughtan is particularly interesting yet not many people have heard of her these days. She was 50 when war broke out; she was a successful writer with several books to her name and was a wealthy woman. Sarah was no stranger to war zones, having been in Rio de Janeiro in Brazil during the 1893 – 1894 bombardment.

She also helped tending the wounded in South Africa during the Boer Wars and in The Balkans during The Balkan Wars.

In September 1914, Sarah travelled to Antwerp in Belgium with Mabel St. Clair Stobart's ambulance unit to tend wounded French and Belgian soldiers. When Antwerp was evacuated, Sarah ordered a special mobile kitchen from Harrods in London and had it sent over so she could set up a soup kitchen in northern France. Sarah noticed the plight of wounded French and Belgian soldiers who were often left for days without attention in stations waiting for treatment because the most seriously wounded were tended to first.

After a speaking tour of England, Scotland and Wales, Sarah went to help out in Russia and Persia (now called Iran) in September 1915. During that time she continued to write books and have them published. Sarah returned to England exhausted and ill and died on 24th July 1916.

In sponsoring these Most Valued Player Awards, I wanted to make sure that Sarah's name was remembered."

You can read more about Sarah MacNaughtan and other fascinating women on Lucy's Inspirational Women website at:
http://inspirationalwomenofww1.blogspot.com/2016/1 2/sarah-broome-macnaughtan-1864-1916.html

*– and follow Lucy's "Poet In Residence" Facebook page at **www.facebook.com/lucy-poet-in-residence**.*

9th December 2018 - Women's Premier League
Widnes Wild Women's team 1 - Whitley Bay Squaws 9

Squaws' Amy Moran and Wild's Vicky Venables receive the MVP awards
from sponsor Lucy London (Photos by Paul Breeze)

20th January 2019 - Women's Premier League
Widnes Wild Women's team 3 - Nottingham Vipers 9

Vipers' Alice Haddleton and Wild's Laura Marcroft receive the MVP awards
from sponsor Lucy London (Photos by Geoff White)

10th February 2019 - Women's Premier League
Widnes Wild Women's team 2 - Chelmsford Cobras 8

Cobras' Rosie Wallace and Wild's Katie Adshead receive the MVP Award
from sponsor Lucy London (Photo by Geoff White)

10th March 2019 - Women's Premier League
Widnes Wild Women's Team 1 - Milton Keynes Falcons 4

Falcons' team captain Kirsten Noble receives the MVP award from Shannon
Holt Wild 's Stephanie Drinkwater receives the Widnes MVP from Lucy
London (Photos by Paul Breeze)

7th April 2019 - Women's Premier League
Widnes Wild Women's Team 2 - Bracknell Firebees 14

Firebees' Emily Harris and Wild's Elizabeth Loss receive the MVP awards from sponsor Lucy London (Photos by Paul Breeze)

28th April 2019 - Women's Premier League
Widnes Wild Women's Team 1 - Kingston Diamonds 13

Diamonds' Ketziah Robinson receives the Kingston MVP award from Mandy Sinclair and Wild women's Daisy Lloyd-Hazlegreaves receives the Widnes MVP award from Lucy London (Photos by Geoff White)

19th May 2019 - Women's Premier League
Widnes Wild Women's Team 0 - Sheffield Shadows 8

Sheffield's Leah Cheetham and Wild's Charlotte McPhee receive the MVP awards from Poet In Residence Lucy London (Photos by Paul Breeze)

Edith Smith Memorial MVP Awards
Widnes Wild Women's Ice Hockey Team Season 2019/20

https://edithsmithmemorialawards.blogspot.com/

September 2019: Edith Smith MVP Awards Launched at First Home Game

The Edith Smith Memorial MVP Awards for the Widnes Wild Women's Team 2019/2020 Season were launched at the first home game on Sunday, 22nd September 2019 at Planet Ice, Widnes.

Edith became Britain's first ever Warranted Woman Police Officer during the First World War and Lucy London – Poet in Residence at the Planet Ice Rink in Widnes, Cheshire, UK – decided that she would like to commemorate Edith and name the MVP Awards for the 2019/2020 Season in her honour.

Inspector Victoria Holden and Superintendent Louise Harrison of Merseyside Police had been instrumental in ensuring that Edith had a proper headstone.

Sponsors meet some of the players before the game (left to right): Victoria Holden ,Lucy London, Louise Harrison, Bob Knowles, Carolyne Knowles. Players left to right: Catherine Bowen-Fell, Emma Pearson, Sav Sumner, Kat Garner. (Photo by Paul Breeze).

And they, along with Wirral Historian Bob Knowles, were invited to the match to help launch the Award. They all met some of the players before the game and Inspector Holden and Superintendent Harrison presented the match puck to get proceedings off to a flying start.

Bob Knowles has written a book about Edith and brought some copies along, together with some interesting items about Edith to display during the match. Bob presented the MVP Awards at the end of what turned out to be a very entertaining and exciting game.

After the game, Bob - from the Oxton Historical Society - said: *"I'm extremely glad you invited me to the match. It was an absolutely splendid experience. I spent the whole match standing up so that I could see all the action. Everybody was very welcoming and it was, I'll have to say, an unforgettable experience."*

Bob Knowles' book is called "Edith Smith - Britain's First Warranted Policewoman" and can be purchased from both The Oxton Historical Society and Grantham Civic Society, price £3.

Inspector Victoria Holden and Superintendent Louise Harrison present the match puck to Captains Karen Craig of Solway and Emma Pearson of Widnes, respectively. (Photo by Paul Breeze).

22nd September 2019 - Challenge Match
Widnes Wild Women 8 - Solway Sharks Ladies 8

Wirral Historian Bob Knowles presents the MVP awards to Solway's
Kimberley Breingan and Wild's Catherine Fell. (Photos by Paul Breeze).

6th October 2019 - WNIHL Div 1 North
Widnes Wild Women 7 - Sheffield Shadows 2

Sheffield Shadows' Shannon Schneider and Wild women's netminder
Stephanie Drinkwater receive the MVP awards from junior mascot Jacob
Downe and match volunteer Lauren Holt (Photos by Paul Breeze)

15th December 2019 - WNIHL Div 1 North
173

Widnes Wild Women 9 - Solway Sharks 5

Solway's Michelle Croucher and Wild's Leen de Decker receive the MVP awards from mascot Corey Miller (Photos by Geoff White)

5th January 2020 - WNIHL Div 1 North
Widnes Wild Women 15 - Nottingham Vipers 1

Vipers' Linaia Trusswell and Wild's Sarah Aspinall receives the MVP awards from Julia Shutt and mascots Lilly Miller and Henry Pearson (Photo by PB)

16th February 2020 - WNIHL Div 1 North
Widnes Wild Women 12 - Grimsby Wolves 2

Wolves' Abbie-Jane Mercer and Wild's Leen de Decker receive the MVP awards from Nicky Jackson (Photo by Paul Breeze)

1st March 2020 - WNIHL Div 1 North
Widnes Wild Women 8 - Telford Wrekin Raiders 1

Raiders' Rachel Logan and Wild's Stephanie Drinkwater receive MVP awards from Julia Shutt and various mascots (Photos by Paul Breeze)

24th July 2021 – Challenge Match
Widnes Wild Women 7 – Caledonia Steel Queens 9

Steel Queens' Mikanshi Ashok and Wild's Kat Garner receive the MVP awards from match timekeeper Rebecca Clayton (Photos by Paul Breeze)

28th August 2021 – Informal Challenge Session
Widnes Wild Women – Firebees

Firebees' Alissa Mailes and Wild's Preston Gennoe receive the MVP awards from timekeeper Rebecca Clayton (Photos by Paul Breeze)

Widnes Wild Ladies Ice Hockey Team
2021/22 WPL Season

https://winifredmabellettsmvpawards.blogspot.com/

November 2021: Widnes Wild Ladies Team To Commemorate WW1 Heroine

The Widnes Ladies team are honouring First World War inspirational woman Winifred Mabel Letts this season, following Wild club Poet In Residence Lucy London's decision to sponsor the Most Valuable Player awards this season in her memory.

It is the third year in a row that Lucy has sponsored the MVP awards for the Wild women's home matches and, in keeping with her other main activity – that of researching and raising awareness of the roles of women in the Great

177

War – Lucy has once again decided to dedicate this year's awards to the memory of another such woman.

Winifred Mabel Letts was born on 10th February 1882 in Salford, Manchester. Her parents were Ernest Frederick Letts, an Anglican church minister and his wife, Mary Isabel, nee Ferrier. After the death of Winifred's father, the family moved to Ireland.

Educated at Abbots Bromley School in Staffordshire, Winifred went on to study at Alexandra College in Dublin. Her career as a writer began in 1907 when the novels "Waste Castle" and "The Story Spinner" were published.

During the First World War, Winifred joined the Volunteer Aid Detachment and worked as a nurse at Manchester Base Hospital.

She then trained as a medical masseuse – that is a physiotherapist in modern parlance – with the Almeric Paget Military Massage Corps. Winifred worked at Army camps in Manchester and Alnwick, Northumberland during WW1.

Talking about her choice of Letts to commemorate for this season's awards, Lucy said;

"As the Wild club have a connection with the Physio Department at Salford University for this season, I felt it appropriate to commemorate Winifred as she was born in Salford and became a medical masseuse – which was the forerunner of physiotherapy."

21st November 2021: Women's Premier League
Widnes Wild Ladies 2 - Nottingham Vipers 3

*Vipers' Sarah Kimber and Wild's Preston Gennoe receive the MVP awards
from match announcer Paul Breeze (Photos by Geoff White)*

2nd January 2022 – Women's Premier League
Widnes Wild Ladies 0 – Kingston Diamonds 9

*Diamonds' Megan Day and Wild's Preston Gennoe receive the MVP awards
from match timekeeper Rebecca Clayton (Photos by Paul Breeze)*

9th January 2022 - Women's Premier League
Widnes Wild Ladies 0 – Sheffield Shadows 9

Shadows' Eleanor Cooper and Wild's Phoebe Patient receive the MVP
awards from match goal judge Lynda Bird (Photos by Paul Breeze)

6th February - Women's Premier League
Widnes Wild Ladies 4 – Chelmsford Cobras 13

Cobras' Tegan Hyatt and Wild's Elizabeth Loss receive the MVP awards
from match mascot Lilly Miller (Photos by Paul Breeze)

20th March 2022 - Women's Premier League
Widnes Wild Ladies 3 – Firebees 7

The MVP awards went to Phoebe Dodd for the Firebees and Laura Marcroft for Widnes - and were presented by match scorer Paul Breeze.

No presentation photos were made available.

Laura Marcroft match action photo (left) by Geoff White

3rd April 2022 - Women's Premier League
Widnes Wild Ladies 4 – Slough Sirens 7

Sirens' Aniko Gaal and Wild's Gemma Brown receive the MVP awards from penalty box judge Trisha Holt (Photos by Paul Breeze)

1st May 2022 - Women's Premier League
Widnes Wild Ladies 0 – Bristol Huskies 20

MVP awards presented to Nora Egri of Bristol and Charlotte Cramps of Widnes - by match timekeeper Thomas Horner (photos by Paul Breeze)

8th May 2022 - Women's Premier League
Widnes Wild Ladies 2 – Milton Keynes Falcons 14

MVP awards presented to Samantha Ruff of MK and Vanessa Crickmore Clarke of Widnes - by match volunteer Rhianna Holt (photo by Paul Breeze)

The Kate Luard Memorial MVP Awards
2022/23 Season Awards for the Widnes Wild Ladies Ice Hockey Team

Widnes Wild women's players (l to r) Ellen Tyrer, Ellie Green and Phoebe Patient with the Kate Luard Memorial MVP trophies for the new season (Photo by Paul Breeze)

October 2022: Kate Luard Memorial MVP Award

The Widnes Wild Ladies team have some impressive new trophies for their Most Valuable Player (MVP) awards at their home games this season thanks to the continued sponsorship of the Wild club's Poet in Residence Lucy London.

This is the fourth year in a row that Lucy has sponsored the MVP awards for the Wild Women's ice hockey team's home matches and, in keeping with her other main activity – that of researching and raising awareness of the roles of women in the Great War - Lucy has once again decided to dedicate this year's awards to the memory of another such woman.

This season's award is in memory of British nurse Kate Luard, RRC and Bar (1872 - 1962)

Born in Aveley, Essex in 1872, Kate was educated at Croydon High School and trained during the 1890s at The East London Hospital for Children, then at King's College Hospital in London. She joined the Army Nursing Service in 1900 and served for two years in South Africa during the Second Boer War (1899 - 1902).

Kate was in her 40s and Matron of the Berks and Bucks County Sanatorium when she joined the Queen Alexandra's Imperial Military Nursing Service on 6th August 1914. She was mobilised and sent to France. For her services as a nurse on the Western Front in WW1, Kate was awarded the Royal Red Cross in 1916 and a bar was added to the award in June 1918.

The Royal Red Cross (RRC) medal was introduced by Queen Victoria on 27th April 1883. The Royal warrant provides for the award "to any ladies, whether subjects or foreign persons, who may be recommended by Our Secretary of State for War for special exertions in providing for the nursing of sick and wounded soldiers and sailors of Our Army and Navy". IN WW1, during the reign of King George V the words 'or Our Air Force in the field' were added.

When used in conjunction with medals awarded for exceptional service, the term "and bar" means that the award has been bestowed several times.

For the 2018/19 season, the Wild women MVP awards were dedicated to the memory of Sarah MacNaughtan, who single-handedly set up and operated soup kitchens in the war zones on the Western Front. In 2019/20, the awards were in honour of Merseyside-born Edith Smith, who became the country's first warranted woman police officer during WW1 and later worked as a nursing assistant at a hospital in Runcorn.

After the break due to Covid, the 2021/22 season, the Wild women MVP awards were dedicated to the memory of Winifred Mabel Letts, British WW1 VAD, writer and poet, who was born in Salford and worked as a Military Masseuse during WW1 at Army camps in Manchester and Alnwick, Northumberland during WW1.

Talking about her choice of Luard to commemorate for this season's awards, Lucy said:

"I decided on Kate Luard for this season as she was one of the WW1 nurses awarded the Royal Red Cross medal. Her bravery was such that she had a Bar added to the RRC medal.

Several years ago, I read the book of Kate's war-time letters in which she described conditions on the Western front and was very impressed. Kate survived the war but many of the nurses were killed or died of illnesses contracted during their service. As we haven't yet commemorated a nurse I felt it was time to do so."

Luard's great-niece Caroline Stevens said of the awards: "Kate would be tickled pink with this!"

You can find out more about Kate Luard's fascinating life and writings on Caroline's dedicated website at: http://kateluard.co.uk/

16th October 2022 – WNIHL Div 2 North
Widnes Wild Women 9 – Whitley Bay Beacons 0

Whitley's Rebecca Boardman and Wild's Lise Gillen receive the MVP awards from match timekeeper Rebecca Clayton (photos by Paul Breeze).

30th October 2022 – WNIHL Div 2 North
Widnes Wild Women 7 – Sheffield Shadows 5

Sheffield's Morgan Ashley and Wild's Lucy Kirkham for Widnes receive the MVP awards from match timekeeper Conner Dakin (Photos by Paul Breeze)

5th January 2023 - WNIHL Div 2 North
Widnes Wild Women 5 – Telford Wrekin Raiders 4

Telford's Tegan Hyatt and Wild's Charlotte Cramp receive the MVP awards from match timekeeper Howard Smith (Photos by Paul Breeze)

5th February 2023 -: WNIHL Div 2 North
DMUK Widnes Wild Ladies 15 - Kingston Diamonds 2

Kingston's Tiya Dhillon and Wild's Karyn Cooper receive the MVP awards from Laura Prescott of Debt Movement UK and her daughter Emily. (Photos by Paul Breeze)

5th March 2023 - WNIHL Div 2 North
DMUK Widnes Wild Women 7 - Grimsby Wolves 2

The MVP awards were presented by match timekeeper Howard Smith and went to Sophie Hill for Widnes and the netminder for Grimsby (Photo by PB)

26th March 2023 – WNIHL Div 2 North
DMUK Widnes Wild Women 0 - Solway Sharks Ladies 6

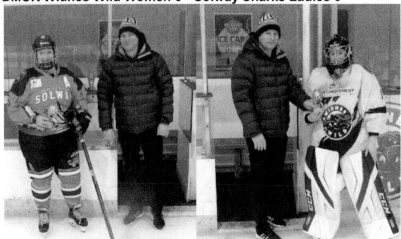

Solway's Rosaline Adey and Wild's Stephanie Drinkwater receive the MVP awards from penalty box judge Andy Patient (Photos by Paul Breeze)

23rd April 2023 – WNIHL Div 2 North
DMUK Widnes Wild Women 9 - Leeds Roses 2

Leeds' Rosie Steedman and Wild's Natalie Buckles receive the MVP awards from penalty box judge Helen Patient (Photos by Paul Breeze).

Pauline Hayward helping to launch the 2019/20 Wild women's MVP awards
(Photo by Paul Breeze)

Pauline Hayward

Sometime ago I posted this little poem on my Facebook page:

"Over the River"

Across the River Mersey my thoughts often float
Drifting and dreaming with the River's flow
Light and happy in an imaginary boat.
Won't you tell me, please where your thoughts go?

LL 18th March 2020

(Inspired by the 1958 DDR song "Uber die Elbe", lyrics by Heribert Klein)

My friend Pauline Hayward, who I met because she played for the Widnes Wild Women's Ice Hockey Team, replied with this delightful verse, so I asked her if we could include it:

Oooh when my mind drifts, it's on ice that I glide,
Frictionless; thrilling, I never collide;
Match day excitement, the ping of a puck; mad ref decisions and slices of luck.
But the wildest of dreams; due to greatest fatigue - nothing compares quite, to winning the league*

Pauline agreed and sent me a bit about herself and some photos for us to use.

"I'd describe myself as "late to the party. Prompted by Sport England's "This Girl Can" programme which sponsored ten weeks of free coaching at Widnes, I learned to skate and began to play ice hockey as a total beginner in my sixties."

"Before I knew it, I was playing with the Widnes Wild ladies, with the best team-mates anyone could ever wish for I've been playing and partying ever since."

"I knew I had gone completely "Wild" when I agreed to join some of the others in Tough Mudder. If there's anything that you have always wanted to do, my advice is "go for it". You'll surprise yourself!"

*(*To the best of our knowledge, Pauline is the oldest ever player to have won a competitive league title when she was a member of the Widnes Wild women's team that won the WNIHL Division 1 North title during the 2019/20 season.)*

Left: Pauline Hayward playing ice hockey for the Widnes Wild women's team (Photo by Copper Tree Photography)

Below: Pauline being similarly energetic in other surroundings.

*Pauline Hayward (#64) in ice hockey action away at Dumfries
(Photo by Copper Tree Photography)*

Pauline's Bitch

There's a player comically known as "Pauline's Bitch"
Out of politeness to him, I won't say which.
But she knocked him flat, across the ice
I bet he won't let THAT happen twice!

PB 22nd July 2023
(Inspired while washing up – taking a break from editing this book...)

Lucy at Old Trafford for the Cricket World Cup in 1999. The West Indies team are hovering in the background... (Photo by Paul Breeze)

Cricket And Ice Hockey!

Some people may think it odd that I am passionate about two very different sports – cricket and ice hockey - and yet, believe it nor not, there are similarities, ie:.

- Cricket bats are made of willow and the first ice hockey sticks were also made of wood.
- In both games the terrain played on is important and needs extremely careful tending.
- Both games require a detailed score being kept during matches.
- In both games the referees/linesmen/umpires give complex hand signals to those keeping score.

- In both games an extremely hard ball/puck is used, which requires careful maintenance and regular inspection and is changed when it becomes unsuitable.
- And spectators are advised to keep their eyes on the ball or puck.

While watching the televised Highlights of the Ashes Test Match at Lord's on Saturday 1st July 2023, one of the commentators mentioned that 'Mayhem' was on the boundary.

But the Mayhem Para Ice Hockey Team had a home game in Widnes that day and could not possibly have been there. So I was inspired to write this poem:

Manchester Mayhem
Are a Para Ice Hockey Team
You can see them play
Home matches at Planet Ice,Widnes on game day
Entry is free
Mayhem matches to see.

LL, 3.7.2023

**England v Australia Ashes 2023 - Marnus
Labuschagne**

What a truly remarkable name
Is that of Aus cricketer Marnus Labuschagne.
However it really can't compare with Ben Stokes,
Joe Root, Jonny Bairstow, Chris Woakes,
Jimmy Anderson and Stuart Broad -
Oh how those English Lions roared
Whenever Stuart Broad scored –
Zak Crawley, Ben Duckett, Harry Brook,
Moeen Ali and Mark Wood,
Or many a famous England cricketing name -
Denis Compton, Alastair Cook, Nasser Hussain,
Dickie Bird, Geoff Boycott and the Bedser twins -
Forgive me but I can't help hoping England wins …

Lucy London, 21 – 22 July 2023

P.S. "I don't like cricket .... I LOVE it!"
And I love Ice Hockey too - what of it?

Jennifer Wilmarth with Lucy and the Pals at Coffee Aroma, Birkenhead, 7th February 2019 (Photo by Paul Breeze)

Lucy, Jennifer, Birkenhead High School, Colorado Avalanche and the Stanley Cup!

Yesterday (7th February 2019) we met Jennifer Wilmarth who came all the way from Colorado in the United States of America, with her cousin, our friend Stanley Kaye, who lives in London.

Stanley is 'The Poppy Man' – it was his idea that we should all go around planting poppies wherever we went in remembrance so that by 2018 there would be a sea of poppies the world over. Jennifer met Bunny and his friends and she immediately called them 'The Crew'.

Here's a poem I wrote about Jennifer's visit:

Jennifer Wilmarth visited us
on Merseyside yesterday -
Jennifer's from Colorado
in the U.S. of A.
With Jennifer was her cousin,
Stanley Kaye, the Poppy Man
Who encourages us to plant poppies
in remembrance when we can.
We went to the Wilfred Owen Story
in Birkenhead's Argyle Street
So WOS founder, Dean Johnson,
Jennifer could meet.

We then went to Coffee Aroma,
where Jennifer met 'The Crew'
Where we had something good to eat
and all had a nice hot brew.
The Crew – so called by Jennifer –
thought she was really lovely
She's beautiful, intelligent
and very, very bubbly.
It's the first time The Crew
met someone from America
And they were well impressed
with their very own Queen – Jennifer.

Note: the above was originally published in "The
Adventures of Bunny, Archie, Alice & Friends" (2019).

A Little Background Information

Our friends Dr. Margaret Stetz, who is the Mae and Robert Carter Professor of Women's Studies and Professor of Humanities at the University of Delaware in America, and Mark Samuels Lasner, a writer and collector of antique books, who is a Research Fellow at the University of Delaware Library, are very supportive of my work, in particular my First World War research but they also liked my poem about my new furry pals.

Margaret wrote:

"Did you know that there is a whole scholarly literature about this sort of anthropomorphizing? I have on my shelf here in Washington a book by Lois Rostow Kuznets, "When Toys Come Alive: Narratives of Animation, Metamorphosis, and Development", that was published in 1994 by no less a press than Yale University's.

So we need not feel the least bit as though we are engaged in anything unusual. There is a long and honoured history behind us. I quote the first sentence from the dust jacket:

"Since the eighteenth century, toys have had an important place in European and American stories written for children and adults, often taking on a secret, sensual, even carnivalesque life of their own."

A Mutual Interest.

While I was talking to Jennifer, I mentioned that Paul and I were interested in ice hockey - and that we helped out at games at Widnes - and she started telling us with great excitement about her local Colorado Avalanche NHL team.

We often exchange presents since we met and Jennifer has sent us a nice selection of Colorado attire.

The Colorado Avalanche team was originally founded as the Quebec Nordiques in Quebec City, Canada, in 1972 but was relocated to Denver, Colorado in 1995.

This new Avalanche NHL "franchise" won the Stanley Cup – the prestigious North American Play Off Trophy - in their first season in 1995/96, again in 2000/01 and for the third time in 2021/22 – and Jennifer was kind enough to send Paul and me tee-shirts celebrating the team's 3rd Stanley Cup triumph.

The Stanley Cup

The background to the Stanley Cup itself is rather interesting and it has a local North West / Liverpool connection.

Commissioned in 1892 and originally called the Dominion Hockey Challenge Cup, the trophy is named after Frederick Arthur Stanley, (1841 – 1908) - Lord Stanley of Preston, 16th Earl of Derby - who was appointed Governor General of Canada and Commander in Chief of Prince Edward Island on 1st May 1888 until 1893.

During that time, organized ice hockey in Canada was just beginning and only Montreal and Ottawa had anything resembling leagues. Lord **Stanley** donated the trophy as an award for Canada's top-ranking amateur ice hockey clubs. **Stanley**'s sons became avid ice hockey players in Canada, playing in amateur leagues in Ottawa, and Lord and Lady **Stanley** became staunch hockey fans.

The first **Stanley** Cup was awarded in 1893 to Montreal HC, and subsequent winners from 1893 to 1914 were determined by challenge games as well as league games.

Professional teams first became eligible to challenge for the **Stanley** Cup in 1906. In 1915, the two professional ice hockey organizations, the National Hockey Association (NHA) and the Pacific Coast Hockey Association (PCHA), reached a gentlemen's agreement in which their respective champions would face each other annually for the **Stanley** Cup.

After a series of league mergers and folds, it was established as the de facto championship trophy of the NHL in 1926 and then the de jure NHL championship prize in 1947.

Since the 1914–15 season, the Cup has been won a combined 101 times by 18 active NHL teams and five defunct teams.

It was not awarded in 1919 because of a Spanish flu epidemic. Joe Hall, who played for the Montreal Canadiens died on April 4th 1919.

Lucy goes back to Birkenhead High School, June 2014
(Photo by Paul Breeze)

The Girls' Public Day School Trust (GPDST)

The GPDST was founded for the education of girls in 1872 by Maria Grey, her sister Emily Shireff, Lady Henrietta Stanley of Alderley and HRH Princess Louise.

Henrietta Maria Stanley, Baroness Stanley of Alderley (née Dillon-Lee; 21 December 1807 – 16 February 1895), was a British Canadian-born (Halifax, Nova Scotia) political hostess and campaigner for the education of women in England.

She married Edward John Stanley, 2nd Baron Stanley of Alderley, PC (13 November 1802 – 16 June 1869) on 7

October 1826, becoming Baroness Eddisbury when her husband was created a peer in 1848.

Two years later he succeeded to the title Baron Stanley of Alderley.

I was always slow at school and my primary school teachers were convinced I would not pass the 11+ examination to get into our local High School for girls. So they asked my parents if they could enter me for the entrance examination to Birkenhead High School which, at that time, was a member of the GPDST. I managed to pass both examinations and it was decided that I should go to Birkenhead High School.

The houses at BHS were Argyll, Grey, Gurney and Stanley – presumably after the founders of the Trust. I was in Argyll House whose colour was green. My friends were Anita, who was in Stanley House, whose colour was yellow, and Sally, who was in Grey House, whose colour was blue.

The name Stanley with Canadian connections was therefore known to me long before I got into ice hockey and heard about the Stanley Cup.

https://www.gdst.net/about-us/our-history/

To bring this whole saga right up to date and make it topical, you might be interested to know that the Rob Craig Memorial Trophy – named in memory of a, sadly, departed Blackburn amateur ice hockey player – which is awarded to the winners of the Ice Hockey Summer Classic Cup, is an exact replica of the Stanley Cup in both size and shape.

Here is a photo of the Wyre Seagulls winning it in 2018.

And this is us wearing some of the wonderful Colorado goodies that Jennifer Wilmarth has sent us:

Colorado Avalanche 2022 Stanley Cup winners t-shirts – taken at home in July 2023

More Colorado attire taken at the Planet Ice rink in Widnes during 2019 and 2020 (left photo by Andrew Shutt).

And, just to finish off with an ice hockey poem - of a sort - here's an attempt at a Calligramme, as originally made popular by First World War French poet Guillaume Apollinaire, where the words are arranged in shapes rather than formal lines of text, to show images of what they are representing.

When viewed in a certain way, and with a lot of imagination, this could possibly look like a cup (or maybe an avalanche...)!

```
C H A M P S
O   V       T
L   -       A
O   A       N
R   -       L
A   L       E
D   A       Y
O   N
    C U P
    H
    E
```

Lucy London, 3rd August 2023

Also from Lucy London....

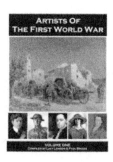
Artists Of The First World War

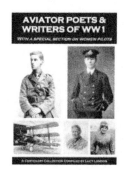
Aviator Poets & Writers

Poets' Corners In Foreign Fields

Female Poets Vol 1

Female Poets Vol 2

No Woman's Land

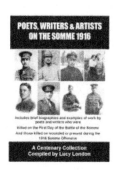
The Somme 1916

Arras, Messines, Passchendaele

Women Casualties – Belgium & France

BOOK REVIEW

I recently received a really lovely gift – a book of poems entitled

"Poems about Cambridge Eskimos & Ice Hockey in the UK"

by Canadian Bill Harris, who is Head Coach of the Cambridge University B Team Cambridge Eskimos, whose home ice pad is at Planet Ice in Peterborough.

(note: since moved to the new Cambridge ice rink)

Professor William "Bill" Harris is Head of the Department of Physiology, Development and Neuroscience at the University of Cambridge, UK, and a Fellow of both the Royal Society and Academy of Medical Sciences.

It is great to see that I am not alone in writing verse about ice hockey.

ISBN: 978-1093829075

Lucy London, June 2019

GUNS & PENCILS

A Collection Of War Poetry

By Lucy London

Published by
Posh Up North Publishing
(5th April 2012)
36 pages paperback
ISBN: 978-0953978229

From visions of the trenches in World War One, right through to modern day conflicts, Lucy London's heart-felt poems fully capture the mood and the emotion of war and all those it affects – and not merely the fighters at the front.

Lucy London has worked for a Mayfair PR agency in London, been a night club DJ in Paris, presented radio shows across Europe and beyond and has written numerous songs, short stories and poems.

This is her first published collection of poetry.

Available from www.poshupnorth.com, Amazon, Kindle, and all other quality outlets…!

PURPLE PATCHES

A Collection Of Poems, Songs and Short Stories From The Fountain Pen of Lucy London.

Published by
Posh Up North Publishing
(1st Feb. 2013)
42 pages paperback
ISBN: 978-1909643000

In this latest compilation of her written works, English poet and songwriter Lucy London shows off her versatility in both subject matter and format.

Here is a collection of poems, short stories - and even some original pieces of artwork - on all manner of different topics from pronunciation to lost love and from cricket to espionage, all produced from the pen and, indeed, the pencil of this highly talented lady.

She writes songs too – but you'll have to wait for another volume of her collected works to savour those little delicacies. In the meantime, why not check this little collection out?

There's something for everybody in here!

Available from www.poshupnorth.com, Amazon, Kindle, and all other quality outlets…!

by Lucy London

THE ADVENTURES OF BUNNY, ARCHIE, ALICE & FRIENDS

By Lucy London

**Independently published (29th Oct. 2019)
32 pages paperback
ISBN: 978-1703634297**

This is a delightful set of little tales told in verse about soft toys Bunny, Archie and Alice and their travels and discoveries around the Wirral Peninsula.

Suitable for adults and children alike.

Available from www.poshupnorth.com, Amazon, Kindle, and all other quality outlets…!

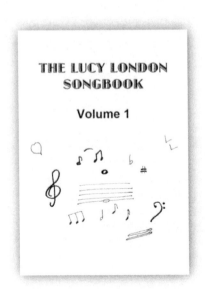

THE LUCY LONDON SONGBOOK
Volume 1

Published by
Posh Up North Publishing
(20th April 2021)
74 pages paperback
ISBN: 978-1909643444

11 original songs written by poet and broadcaster Lucy London - on a variety of different topics and in a variety of different styles. Arranged for voice, piano and guitar chords.

Recording and performance licensing details available upon request.

Available from www.poshupnorth.com, Amazon, Kindle, and all other quality outlets…!

STANLEY CASSON: POEMS & PROSE

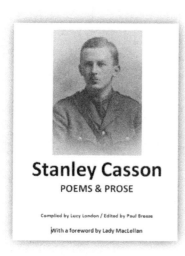

Stanley Casson

POEMS & PROSE

Compiled by Lucy London / Edited by Paul Breeze

With a foreword by Lady MacLellan

Stanley Casson (1889-1944) was never actually a professional soldier – he was by profession an archaeologist and academic - and he only ever donned uniform in time of war to answer the call of his country in the two World Wars of the 20th Century.

This volume represents an overview of the life and writing of Stanley Casson

ISBN: 978-1-909643-50-5

WAR-TIME MEMORIES IN VERSE

By Signaller Frank P Dixon

WAR-TIME MEMORIES IN VERSE

WRITTEN WHILE OVERSEAS
BY SIGNALLER FRANK P DIXON

Originally privately published in 1937 in Canada
by his mother Ellen M Dixon

An annotated and illustrated 2022 reprint with new foreword by Lucy
London, biography, appendices and additional illustrations.

Edited by Paul Breeze

Originally published privately in Canada in 1937 by Dixon's mother, this edition reprinted in 2022 as a centenary reissue, revised and expanded edition with a new foreword, a number of new photographs and illustrations and new additional back pages.

ISBN: 978-1-909643-52-9

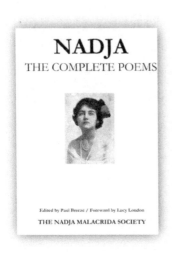

NADJA - THE COMPLETE POEMS

Contents Include:

Armistice day Letter to Nadja 2014
Nadja Malacrida – A Brief Biography
St Dunstan's
The Royal Star & Garter Home
The Evergreen: Poems (1912)
Love And War (1915)
For Empire And Other Poems (1916)
The Full Heart: Poems (1919)

ISBN: 978-1-909643-42-0

WILFRED OWEN: CENTENARY

Contents Include:
Wilfred Owen And Me
Owen Biography In Exhibition Panels
Wilfred Owen In Print
Bullets & Daffodils
Pendle War Poetry Competition
Birkenhead Commemorations
Wilfred Owen Related Sites In Birkenhead 2020

ISBN: 978-1-909643-36-9

WALLASEY - DAYS GONE BY

TONY FRANKS-BUCKLEY

Wirral Historian and writer Tony Franks-Buckley organises The Thursday Evening Myths & Legends Tours in New Brighton, Wirral, UK for people to find out more about the Hidden History of Wallasey.

WALLASEY - DAYS GONE BY

TONY FRANKS-BUCKLEY

Including:

New Brighton Ghosts of the Old Town Tour

Bidston Hill Ghosts, Witches and Folklore Tour

New Brighton Back In Time Tours

The History of The Gunpowder Village and Mother Redcaps Tour

New Brighton Smugglers Trail

For more information and bookings, visit:
https://poulton-creamery.sumupstore.com/

Check out the Facebook page at:
https://www.facebook.com/WallaseyHistoryBook/

Or buy the book via Amazon and elsewhere
ISBN: 978-1481109000

THE TEE ROOM

Where a Tea Room sits side by side with the wonderful world of golf!

172 Banks Road, West Kirby CH48 0RH
Tel: 0151 625 1887 / www.theteeroom.co.uk

The Tee Room is a 24 seater English Tea Room engulfed in a world of golfing bliss and you can find us on Banks Road in West Kirby.

We can seat 24 people and serve everything from breakfasts to traditional afternoon tea. We also have 10 different type of leaf tea, ranging from Traditional English Tea to Lovers Leap & Japanese Green Tea.

You'll always find a warm friendly atmosphere and we pride ourselves on the experience we like to offer our customers.

THE POETS' BENCH
NEW BRIGHTON

A memorial bench for literary contemplation overlooking the River Mersey, docks and Irish Sea.

Street Address: Kings Parade, New Brighton (A554)
Post Code: 86 / CH45 2PB - GPS: 53.436920, -3.067567

New Brighton Promenade is two miles long and, apparently, the longest promenade in England. The Poets' Bench is between exits Promenade 62 and 63 - the numbers are painted on ground by the steps down to the beach.

Lucy London, who began researching the First World War for a series of commemorative exhibitions in 2012, received a donation from a benefactor in America. Following the closure of the Wilfred Owen Story Museum in Argyle Street, Birkenhead, Wirral, Lucy decided to have a First World War Wirral Poets Bench on King's Parade on the Promenade in New Brighton, Wirral, UK. The benches are organised by Wirral Older People's Parliament.

There were quite a few Wirral born or based First World War poets. With the help of Merseyside Historian Debbie Cameron and Liverpool Pals researcher Linda Woodfine Michelini, Lucy recently researched a Wallasey-born WW1 poet – Percy Haselden – who lived in New Brighton and taught art at Wallasey Grammar School.

The Wirral WW1 poets found so far and remembered on the Bench are:

1) Wilfred Owen (1893 – 1918) Born in Shropshire, lived in Birkenhead 1897 – 1907 and used to ride horses on New Brighton beach.

2 WW1 female poet May Sinclair (1863 – 1946) born Mary Amelia St. Clair on 24th August 1863 in Rock Ferry. May joined Dr. Hector Munro's Flying Ambulance Unit as Munro's Personal Assistant and travelled to Belgium with the Unit in September 1914, writing about her experiences on her return to Britain.

3) WW1 aviator poet Geoffrey Wall (1897 – 1917) born Arthur Geoffrey Nelson Wall in Liscard on 3rd March 1897. He lived in Denton Drive, New Brighton and was educated at Seabank Road High School. He joined the Royal Flying Corps in 1915 after going to live in Australia.

4) WW1 soldier poet Reginald Bancroft Cooke (1887 – 1946) born in Birkenhead in 1887. The family lived in Ashville Road, Claughton. He served in WW1 with the Princess Patricia's Canadian Light Infantry after going to live in America.

5) WW1 soldier poet Leonard Comer Wall (1896 – 1917) born in West Kirby, joined the West Lancashire Royal Field Artillery & was killed in June 1917. He left money for his horse Blackie to be repatriated. Blackie lived until 1942 and died at the age of 35 in the RSPCA facility in Hunts Cross, Liverpool - still bearing scars of the shrapnel that killed his master.

6) WW1 poet Olaf Stapledon (1886 – 1950) born in Egremont, as a conscientious objector he joined the Friends' Ambulance Unit

and served in France from July 1915 to January 1919. Awarded the French Croix de Guerre. He lived in Caldy – Stapledon Wood is named in his memory.

7) Percy Haselden (1886 – 1959) poet, teacher and artist. Born Percy Haselden Evans, Liscard. Lived in "End Cliff", Wellington Road, New Brighton in 1911. Art Master Wallasey Grammar School 1909 – 1920.

8) Celia, Lady Congreve (1867 – 1952) – British poet and WW1 nurse. Lived Burton Hall, Burton, nr Neston. Served Belgium & France; awarded Croix de Guerre, Reconnaissance Française & Belgian Medaille de la Reine Elisabeth for bravery for being one of the last nurses to leave Antwerp with the wounded in 1914. French Croix de Guerre for her bravery as a nurse at Rosières-aux-Salines, near Nancy, France. The hospital was shelled and bombed by aircraft in 1918.

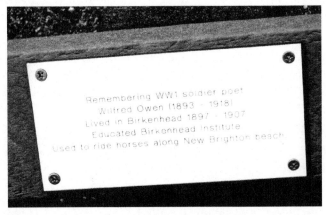

 Follow on Facebook:
The Poets' Bench New Brighton

ICE HOCKEY
REVIEW
www.icehockeyreview.co.uk

Oxside Flyers
A COMPLETE RECORD
SEASONS 2011/12 & 2012/13

THE SEAGULL HAS LANDED!

A LIGHT-HEARTED REVIEW OF THE FIRST 12 WINTERS BACK TOGETHER OF THE BLACKPOOL SEAGULLS ICE HOCKEY TEAM

ICE HOCKEY (1936)
by Major BM Patton
Annotated & Illustrated 2020

A facsimile reprint of the original 1936 edition with new introduction, author biography and appendices

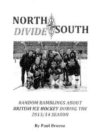

NORTH DIVIDE SOUTH

RANDOM RAMBLINGS ABOUT BRITISH ICE HOCKEY DURING THE 2013/14 SEASON

By Paul Breeze

NORTH / SOUTH DIVIDE

Volume 2: Ice Hockey And Me

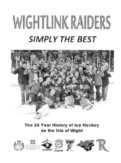

WIGHTLINK RAIDERS
SIMPLY THE BEST

The 25 Year History of Ice Hockey on the Isle of Wight

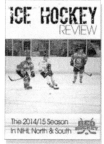

ICE HOCKEY REVIEW
The 2014/15 Season In NIHL North & South

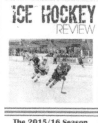

ICE HOCKEY REVIEW
The 2015/16 Season In NIHL North & South

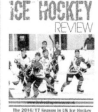

ICE HOCKEY REVIEW
The 2016/17 Season in UK Ice Hockey

ICE HOCKEY REVIEW
THE UK HOCKEY YEARBOOK 2018

Available by mail order from www.poshupnorth.com, Amazon, icehockeyreview.co.uk and other quality outlets

Printed in Great Britain
by Amazon

27754844R00126